A PASSION FOR PLANNING

Financials, Operations, Marketing, Management, and Ethics

Gina Vega

University Press of America,® Inc.
Lanham New York Oxford

Copyright © 2001 by
University Press of America,® Inc.
4720 Boston Way
Lanham, Maryland 20706

12 Hid's Copse Rd.
Cumnor Hill, Oxford OX2 9JJ

Library of Congress Cataloging-in-Publication Data

Vega, Gina.
A passion for planning : financials, operations, marketing,
management, and ethics / Gina Vega.
p. cm
Includes bibliographical references and index.
l. Business planning. I. Title.
HD30.28 .V43   2000   658.4'012—dc21   00-048854 CIP

ISBN 0-7618-1853-7 (cloth : alk. ppr.)
ISBN 0-7618-1854-5 (pbk. : alk. paper)

⊖™The paper used in this publication meets the minimum
requirements of American National Standard for Information
Sciences—Permanence of Paper for Printed Library Materials,
ANSI Z39.48—1984

For Robert
who has shared my passions for thirty-five years

Contents

Foreword

Another "how to" book for business plans! Do we really need another one? There are already so many on the market and, with few minor exceptions, they recommend the same considerations, in the same language, and in the same categories.

We need this one for several reasons, and all of them have to do with context. For the most part, business-plan books abstract business not only from the persons involved in its establishment and growth, but also from the local and global communities. They readily assume that the business will be a self-contained entity, detached from the world in which it is to be created and sustained. They also assume that the business enterprise can be expressed in a mathematical formula with all of the numbers yielding a clear, neat, precise summation we readily accept as conclusive and definitive.

Gina Vega makes no such assumptions. She challenges the entrepreneur to take stock, to examine one's motives and objectives, and to question one's values and ethics: What is important? What is important to me, to the people who will be providing and receiving goods and services? What is important now, and what will be important in the future? How do I make money and, at the same time, enrich my life and the lives of people around me? Underlying her recommendations is a refreshingly positive and engaging appreciation of business, and of men and women in business. It is nothing less than, as the title indicates, a matter of passion for life and business in all of its dimensions.

Important to her is that business—any business—is necessarily contextualized within an interconnecting matrix of relationships—with oneself, with other people, with nature and the cosmos, with the totality of experience and reality. Nothing can be ignored; no one can be dismissed. The context in which a business is established and grown is nothing less than the entirety and totality of life and work.

It would be a mistake, then, to read this book and assess its recommendations in the usual linear, developmental way to which we have become accustomed. Creating and sustaining a business involves more than a series of building blocks stacked one on top of another. That is especially true if those blocks are labeled numerically and alphabetically, and categorized as distinct ingredients disconnected from one another.

Creating a business plan is, for Vega, more than simply a matter of following a recipe to make sure all of the ingredients are accounted for and measured. Cajun cooking, for example, requires that, "first, you make a roux," the equal portions of flour and oil, cooked on a stove top, preferably in an iron pot, stirred for hours, until thickened and browned, required for any good gumbo. Later, as spices are blended into the roux, the gumbo begins to assume character and definition. As oysters, shrimp, and crabs (or chicken and sausage) are added to the mix that definition becomes even more pronounced.

When placed before us, our senses are awakened to the whole of the gumbo. In each spoonful we see, taste, and smell something of its totality. We might want to know what that totality represents and how the gumbo came before us, and question how the roux was made, or what spices went into it. We might even want someone to give us the recipe and explain the procedures for achieving the end result.

Gina Vega is interested in recipes and procedures. She knows they're important. However, she is even more interested in the underlying motives leading to the end result, especially those that cannot be contained in simple formulae, recipes, or precise definitions. She is asking why anyone would go through all this time and energy in the first place, and how that driving motivation is expressed in any and every function of the business.

The word "integration" comes to mind, but not in its secondary connotation of tying everything together in a logical, consistent whole. In this book, integration is a matter of identifying that one operative principle underlying the many connections and interconnections, even those we can't readily define and categorize. It is a matter of acknowledging the whole before any of its parts, and of realizing that the whole cannot be confined to the limits of time and space, or the limits of mathematical precision. It is precisely this tendency to reduce business to dollars and cents that Vega is urging us to transcend.

The contemporary novelist Mary Gordon is questioning those same tendencies when writing a biography of Joan of Arc. She is recommending a perspective of integration similar to Vega's:

> If I could, I would begin this study in a way that would defy the limits of space and time. I call it a study, or a meditation, hesitating over the honorable term *biography*, with its promise of authority, of scholarship, of scope and sweep. Ideally, I would present you not with pages, but with an envelope of paper strips, each with some words written on it, and a series of snapshots. I would have you open the envelope, drop the strips and photographs on the floor, then pick them up and read them in whatever order they had arranged themselves in your hand. I would require, then, that you replace the strips in the envelope and empty them again. And pick them up again. And read and look again. And again, and again, giving pride of place to no one order.[i]

When Vega enjoins us to develop a sound and accurate financial plan for the business, she does not want us to focus so intently on making the numbers work that we ignore consideration of their impact on operations, marketing, management, or ethics. True, each of these aspects of the business needs to be researched, studied, and projected as a distinct function. That function, however, cannot be pursued as a self-contained unit and placed along side other functions (as many business plans suggest) as so many variables in a formula or ingredients in a recipe. Rather, the financial plan is one aspect of the whole with all kinds of implications and consequences for the other functions of the business.

Analogously, Joseph A. Barry appeals to the world of art, and to Paul Cezanne's injunction to "treat nature by the cylinder, the sphere, and the cone" as if to say "treat business by the finances, operations, marketing, and management." But, as there is more to nature than Cezanne's threesome, there is also more to business than this foursome. "Why not treat nature by the cube" as well, suggests Barry, continuing to explain how, "under the impact of Picasso, Braque, and Gris, cubism was born."[ii] Inherent to nature is cylinders, spheres, cones, *and* cubes. Inherent to business is finances, operations, marketing, management, *and* ethics. To ignore them is to ignore the totality of the business enterprise.

Throughout this book, Vega appeals to those connections both implicitly and explicitly, and wants us to do the same. She wants us to experience any one action or transaction as a microcosm of the whole business, as expressive of an integration of policy and procedure, motive and direction encompassing a whole range of important considerations we usually ascribe to values.

What does she mean by values, and why does she want us to include an ethical audit along with financial, operations, marketing, and management audits? She is suggesting that ethics are not simply important considerations for business, standing alongside other important considerations. She is claiming that, whether acknowledged or not, the values driving motivation and objective are reflected in every business transaction, internal and external. What is important for owners becomes absorbed by managers and workers, and becomes activated in relationships with suppliers and retailers.

Vega is not referring to ethics simply as a listing of DOs and DON'Ts, or a set of rules governing conduct and behavior, whether formal or informal. Rather, ethics are reflective and expressive of the identity and culture of the business. Neither are ethics confined to conventional injunctions against lying, cheating, or stealing. Ethics are expressions of the values driving the business enterprise as a whole, and also driving its relationships with all of its stakeholders, even those that cannot be readily identified.

She would agree with Mary Gordon, then, that ethics, like life itself, cannot be simply ordered around static codes of conduct and behavior. They must be constantly reevaluated and reassessed, as would any other function of the business. Everyone connected with the business would have to "read and look again. And again, and again, giving pride of place to no one order." And, do so unceasingly and unsparingly.

Until you felt that you had understood something in a way that refused finality. That you could tolerate an understanding that allows that the fragments can be endlessly reordered, must be, and that the sense of knowing is always temporary, subject to revision, reversal, recombination, and a relaxation of the compulsion to know what is unknowable.[iii]

For us as individual persons, or for a business as a corporate person, there is a need for constant reinterpretation and reassessment, for always asking the question, "What is really driving me?" Studying the American Dream, Tim Kasser and Richard M. Ryan reached the conclusion that we answer that question with respect to two differing, and opposing, sets of values: money, fame, and image, on the one hand,[iv] and affiliation (relatedness), community feeling (helpfulness), physical fitness (health), and self-acceptance (growth), on the other. [v]

Of the two, the first set has assumed dominance, and is readily acknowledged and pursued as primary, in business and in business plans. To ascertain the accuracy of that conclusion, we need only assess the extent to which most business plans direct us to concentrate on money, fame, and image while virtually neglecting helpfulness, health, and growth. Actually, what we often find is that the second set of values is relegated to the periphery, and considered only insofar as it contributes to or deflects from achieving money, fame, and image. In Herbert Stein's words, underlying business plans is "the expectation of being enriched largely by the efforts of others."[vi]

The real contribution of this book is that it gives equal weight to both sets of values, and invites entrepreneurs and managers to expand their scope of knowledge to appeal to its rational and affective dimensions in creating and growing their businesses. For Vega, it is not a matter of "either/or" but of "both/and." When assessing our values, and our ethics, we want to pay attention to both, equally and unrelentingly, and to assess our finances, operations, marketing, management, and ethical functions with respect to both. We want to be enriched, but also to enrich others.

She is recommending that we pay equal attention to our own self-interests and to others-interests. She is recommending that any business does the same, and assesses and reassesses its internal and external transactions with respect to both. To do otherwise will incur lost opportunities, and those lost opportunities will incur lost revenues. We need only refer to the exorbitant fines levied on companies for polluting the air or the water, or the huge sums awarded to men and women claiming harassment to make that case.

There is also throughout the book, and throughout her recommendations, the futility of pursuing one set of values to the detriment of the other. Pursuing self-interest to the extreme results ultimately in individualistic and corporate selfishness and greed. Pursuing others-interest results in altruism so pervasive that we lose sight of our own identities. No, Vega wants both sets of values to enter into decision-making, and to be weighed equally when structuring finances, operations, marketing, management, and ethics.

If, as we often hear, "information is power," then that information should encompass the whole range of human values, and, in the final analysis, success or failure will hinge on our doing so, as well as on the manner in which we bring both sets of values into play. It is a matter of informing ourselves about ourselves, and of assessing our motives, and of identifying the values inherent to those motives.

Within this book, Vega is saying something very important. She is asking us to move beyond the expected and the ordinary, to push the envelope, to think about ourselves and our businesses in ways surpassing the limitations and boundaries of the expected. She is asking us to do that especially in constructing business plans.

As that one spoonful of gumbo contains the totality of its roux, spices, and seafood, so does any one single business transaction express the totality of its finances, operations, marketing, management, and ethics. Aware of this herself, Vega enjoins us to broaden our own awareness, and from the moment of inception, to assume a perspective of integrated totality in creating and growing businesses.

Pat Primeaux, S.M.
St. John's University
June, 2000

---

[i] Mary Gordon, *Joan of Arc* (New York: Viking, 2000), xxiv.

[ii] Joseph A. Barry, *Left Bank Right Bank: Paris and Parisians* (New York: W.W. Norton & Company, 1951), 152.

[iii] Mary Gordon, *Joan of Arc* (New York: Viking, 2000), xxiv.

[iv] Tim Kasser and Richard M. Ryan, "A Dark Side of the American Dream: Correlates of Financial Success as a Central Life Aspiration," *Journal of Personality and Social Psychology*, 65:2, 1993, 410-422.

[v] Tim Kasser and Richard M. Ryan, "Furthering Examining the American Dream: Differential Correlates of Intrinsic and Extrinsic Goals," *Personality and Social Psychology Bulletin,* 22:3, March, 1996, 280-291.

[vi] Herbert Stein, "The American Dream," *Wall Street Journal,* December 24, 1996, A-8.

Preface

──────────────────➤

It's great fun to work with students and small business owners because they often share a delightful trait – they are motivated by a vision of what *could* be, rather than allowing themselves to be limited by what already *is*.   That enthusiasm is the foundation for building great businesses and great minds.

But enthusiasm alone will not carry the day – a method is needed to create structure out of confusion, strategy out of opportunity, and profit out of dreams, while maintaining a socially responsible attitude and concern for others in the marketplace.

As businesses grow and evolve, the plan that guides them needs to keep pace with the changing company. Too often, a business plan languishes on a shelf, unrevised, to be trotted out and tarted up when money is being sought. This book focuses on existing small businesses and looks specifically at the ethics of organization that guide their development.

There are important reasons to keep business plans current and reflective of a company's stage of development. Small businesses pass through three main stages of development during their normal life cycle (startup, growth, and maturity); the business plan serves different purposes during each of these stages.

An entrepreneur may falter after the first or second year in business, while trying to make the transition from startup to growth. A current and working plan can help the small business owner make this transition from one stage to the next. A startup company will often have the search for funding as its primary business plan focus. This search can successfully force the founder to articulate clearly the vision that will drive the emergent firm. A company in the growth stage is likely to use its plan to formalize processes and guide management in establishing a sense of order after the chaos inherent in startup. And a mature company will use the business plan to review accomplishments and redirect or refocus in order to continue its success in a changing environment.

This book provides four tools to the reader:

(1)   a three-dimensional matrix that clarifies which sections of the business plans should be emphasized at the three main stages of business development in eight different industries,

(2)   examples of "live" business plans in these industries, developed and used by small business owners today,

(3)   commentaries on these plans by functional specialists and industry experts who have evaluated the plans in the context of the businesses,

(4)   an extensive set of resources and references, electronic, hard copy, and human, to assist in business plan development.

The unique focus on real, live business plans written by small business owners rather than consultants – a "warts and all" approach to business planning – will both comfort and challenge you to examine the direction your business is heading.

Although most books about business planning are about how to *write* a plan, this book is about how to *use* the plan to aid in a company's growth. This tool will help you to focus your efforts more closely on areas that will enhance your long-term success, and guide you in imagining your business plan as integral to sustaining growth and personal transformation rather than only as a fund raising mechanism. In the words of one reader, "If I had had this book 10 years ago, I could have avoided a lot of agonizing over my business."

I hope that you will enjoy a look at the intimate details of existing businesses, at Tom's of Maine original "back of the envelope" plan, which demonstrates the potential of a big success from a small start, and at the insightful commentaries from industry experts.

But most importantly, I hope that the planning matrix that shows at a glance what to emphasize in a plan, both by industry and by corporate developmental stage, will help you to employ contingent planning to differentiate needs in a range of situations, and that the ethical subtext that underlies the recommendations in this book will guide you toward a broader view of organizational success and achievement.

Acknowledgments

$\longrightarrow$

No author writes a book alone. There are always many people whose contributions are integral to the success of a writing project; this project is no different. *A Passion for Planning* is the result of the willing and generous contributions of both business owners and business analysts, experts in their fields.

Nearly all of the names and locations of businesses and owners featured in this book have been disguised to protect their privacy and financial interests. All the business owners openly shared financial and personnel information with me, despite the sensitive nature of these items. Although I cannot thank them by name, I very much appreciate their generosity, kindness, and trust in me. Two businesses have not requested anonymity – Tom's of Maine and Dynachrome, Inc. I wish to acknowledge the special commitment that Tom Chappell and Dave Ferrairo have shown, as models of social responsibility, to the goals of furthering education.

The business analysts, colleagues and friends all, who provided the insightful and wise commentary about the featured business plans taught me a great deal, and were a pleasure to work with. Greg Simpson, who wrote the sample plan in Chapter 2, is to be commended for his creativity and technically excellent design. Alexis Vega-Singer performed the yeoman's task of proofreading and copy editing (although any errors that remain in the text are my own responsibility). And, for his patient reading and re-reading of revision after revision, his listening to interminable discussions over a single word or the formatting of a page, for always keeping my electronic powder dry, for his realistic suggestions and uncomplaining endurance, I thank my husband, Robert.

Gina Vega
Haverhill, MA
September, 2000

Chapter 1

———————————————➤

Your Business Plans – Use 'Em to Raise $$; Use 'Em to Grow Your Business

According to a recent study of U.S. business owners[i], more than 75 percent of small business owners have a plan, whether it is in their heads or more formally written down. But we can hardly classify 75 percent of small businesses "successful." What is it about these "good" business plans that differentiate them from the rest? What makes a business plan effective?

This book shares live business plans gathered from entrepreneurs across the United States in order to answer those questions for you. These small business owners have developed their own plans, mostly without professional assistance, and have used them to guide their companies' growth.

Although generally successful as a group, some of the businesses in this book have faltered. In fact, none of these businesses has had an easy ride; that's just not how small business works. Ups and downs are typical of small businesses early in their life cycle, with stability only arriving as the company matures[ii]. The plans in this book reflect the different needs a business has at various life cycle stages. No matter what stage your business is in, from the germ of an idea through a mature company in a mature industry, you'll be able to find a plan here that touches a chord for you.

However, you will not find one special format to follow when designing your own business plan. No hard and fast rules, no specialized formats, no required structures, or magic vitamins will resolve your business planning challenges. There are many excellent volumes that can guide you in the actual writing and design of your business plan; I have listed several excellent choices in Chapter 11 for you to refer to.

But this book has a different goal. Let us presume that your interest fits one or more of the following categories:

1. You currently own a small business and want to expand it, so you are seeking funding or investors.
2. You are thinking of purchasing an existing business and want to analyze its current business plan.
3. You are a potential entrepreneur and want to look at some real plans that might help you create your own.
4. You are a student of entrepreneurship and want to learn about how small businesses use their plans to guide growth and development.
5. You are interested in comparing your plan to others in your industry to see the differences and similarities and to establish some benchmarks.
6. Your professional advisors have wisely reminded you that business planning is a dynamic process, and the plan you wrote when you were green is not serving you today.

You can refer to the plans in this book for inspiration, guidance, comparison, and insight. The small business owners who wrote the plans that appear here are not professional business plan writers, so some of what you will see may appear awkward or amateurish. That is exactly what makes these plans so valuable. They have not been sanitized, homogenized, or whitewashed -- these are real plans, written by people who love their businesses (an "amateur" is, after all, someone who loves a particular endeavor). These plans are like your own plans.

Each plan incorporates a commentary, critique, or analysis by an industry specialist or functional expert. The experts point out some strong and weak areas of the plans, and make it clear what stage of business development the plan would be used for. Some of these plans describe the state of a particular business at the present time, some the original startup condition of the business, and others the business the owner would like to grow into. They might accurately represent the current financial or organizational status of the businesses, or they might reflect a more optimistic view of the business than exists. No one ever describes a business pessimistically, at least not in the many plans I have read!

A plan is not for everyone. Some of the plans' writers claimed that their business plan was a good guide for development, while others claimed that it had little or no effect on their businesses. A third, much smaller group found no use for their plans once they were written. In fact, some very successful, high profile businesses have been established without any written plans. They have even attracted private investors without a plan.

You do not need to write a business plan if:

- You are investing your own money and do not expect to borrow or obtain financing from anyone else *or*
- Your company is a hobby rather than a money-making business, so its demise would have no negative effect on you *and*
- Your employees are also enjoying your hobby and not depending on it for their livelihood.

Because money is the fuel that keeps your organization running, not even not-for-profit organizations or social service providers are exempt from the responsibility for making money. As a general rule, making money doesn't "just happen." It requires forethought and planning.

On another level, in order for your business to be successful, it needs to attain the goals you have set for it. Those goals may not be fiscal, as in the case of a non-profit or a small foundation. However, these kinds of companies still have goals to meet and a mission to fulfill.

Who has made the decisions about critical issues like goals and mission? And how have the decisions been communicated to employees, investors, assistants, and other interested and involved parties? How is the business actually supposed to work? The entrepreneurs who design and the owners who manage these businesses are responsible for the mission, the goals, and the means of implementation. They need to make their purpose clear.

The main value in building your business by using a business plan is that, for most people, knowing where you are going and having an idea about how to get there greatly increases the likelihood of actually arriving at the destination. And, for most people, getting money to finance the adventure requires documentation, thought, focus, and effort -- in other words, a plan. One of the goals of this book is to show you how you can use your plan so that it becomes an asset rather than a drain on your energies.

Defining Terms

Before we move forward, we need to clarify two important terms. An obvious place to start might be:

- *What is a business plan?*

A business plan is a description of your business and how you intend to make it successful. Short, sweet, and simple. Chapter 2 is devoted to expanding and clarifying this definition.

■   *What is the business life cycle?*

The life cycle of a business has three main stages: start-up, the growth phase, and maturity. We talk about these business developmental stages as if they represented stages of human life. We can relate start-up to childhood, the growth phase to adolescence, and maturity to full adulthood. This convention may make it easier to accept the range of behaviors or actions, attitudes, and measurable characteristics (structure) of a business at each stage.

When we talk about companies at certain stages of business development, we make a number of assumptions. The following chart compares observable characteristics (structure), organizational attitudes, and common behaviors or actions that many businesses experience or display. The descriptors are *often*, but *not always*, accurate for a specific company.

	Start-Up	**Growth**	**Maturity**
Structure	• Few employees (small size) • Limited financial resources • Simple structure, centered around the owner	• Medium to large employee base. ("large" is a relative term. A small business can have a large employee base *for the type of business that it is,* and still be a small business. For example, the average number of workers employed by the *1995 Inc. 500 Fastest Growing* companies was 118, larger than the 100 employee cutoff that is often	• Structure becomes highly defined and formalized (bureaucratic) • Employee base grows more rapidly than production may warrant. • Funding becomes comparatively easy to obtain, as a result of corporate stability.

	Start-Up	Growth	Maturity
Structure		used for small business, but considerably smaller than the 500-employee cutoff that the Small Business Administration uses to differentiate a small business. In this context, "large"means significantly larger than a start-up). • considerable financial activity (not necessarily profitable) and access to deeper pockets when necessary • structure is more complex and is centered around functions, but it remains fluid	
Attitudes	• informal • few policies or established procedures • "anything" goes	• more formality • rules and some established procedures guide decision-making • communication channels begin to form; the free-for-all is over	• policies and procedures are well-established and formal • "chain of command" becomes a way of life • following the rules may be rewarded more than innovation

A Passion for Planning

	Start-Up	Growth	Maturity
Actions	business design setting up tasks/ services/ products establishment of a distribution system pulling together resources, suppliers, vendors, consultants, lenders	• focus is on increasing production, sales, and profits while minimizing expenses • operating systems are refined • "management" becomes distinct from ownership	• diversification of products or purchase of other businesses • geographic expansion of the business • increase in administrative actions

These three basic life cycle stages and their associated activities, structure, and interactions require different planning treatments and adaptive strategies in order to succeed. In the rest of this book, we will examine how a business plan needs to change to reflect the demands of businesses in transition.

Our definition of a business plan as "a description of your business and how you intend to make it successful," seems not to differ in any substantial way from the definition of planning in general: "a method for achieving an end," according to Webster[iii].

Planning implies the ability to recognize opportunities when they appear and making advance preparation that takes advantage of them. And that is exactly why you need to have a business plan -- to sharpen your senses about what might constitute an opportunity for you, and how you will exploit the opportunities that present themselves.

A business plan is also about creating opportunities and transforming them into concrete successes. The real value of a business plan may lie more in the process of assembling it, the self-examination and assessment of capabilities that the assembly implies, than in the finished product.

Sure, you can use your business plan to obtain financing. But the other uses of the plan are at least as valuable as this one.

✓ Your plan will force you to examine your markets -- Are they sufficient to support the product or service you provide? Are they growing or shrinking? What new markets might you be able to satisfy? What new markets could you create? What percentage of the market can you wrest from your competitors?

✓ Your plan will require you to consider your management team, your sales force, your administrative personnel -- all your employees. Who is representing you in the marketplace? What skills does your group have in abundance, and what is lacking? How can you fill the void? What will your staffing requirements be in a best case/worst case scenario? How will you go about fulfilling them?

✓ Your plan will encourage a thorough analysis of your operations. How does the work get done? What sort of systems are guiding production or delivery of service? What is your product's or service's competitive advantage? How do you intend to improve upon it?

✓ Your plan will demand a full accounting of your financial position -- what you have, what you expect to have, and how you intend to get it.

This book can help you examine your own business plan with an eye to using it to improve your business as it develops. You will learn how to analyze a plan to determine whether it is serving a purpose right now or whether sections of it could benefit from elaboration, expansion, rethinking, or simply rewriting.

You will learn how to use your plan to expand your markets, redesign your operations, refine your product/service offerings, redefine your competition, and seek financing for expansion, purchase, or start-up.

Chapter 2 provides a system that pinpoints where you can focus your energies if your company is in a particular industry at a specific stage of its life cycle. A matrix will guide you in deciding which areas are most critical for your company today, and a generic business plan will provide some guidelines for improvements and suggestions for inclusion.

Chapters 3 through 10 include relevant sections of live business plans, plans that their owners continue to adapt to their current needs. Each plan illustrates a different planning purpose, and is preceded by background information and a set of questions you can ask yourself about the condition of your current plan. Each is followed by a commentary by members of the team of experts I have assembled and an epilogue that provides a corporate update. The team of experts is described in detail in Appendix C.

Chapter 3, "Manufacturing: A Better Mousetrap," features the early plan of a well-known entrepreneur, Tom Chappell, founder of Tom's of Maine. You will see how he made it big from humble beginnings.

Chapter 11 includes an extensive business planning bibliography and a list of resources and sources of assistance for small business owners.

Before you begin, let's consider a familiar palindrome, a phrase that reads the same both forwards and backwards:

→ a)   a man, a plan, a canal, Panama

← b)   amanap, lanac a, nalp a, nam a

What's the message for successful business planning in this palindrome?

It's this: read forward or backwards, your plan must deliver the same coherent message. It may not "look right" to the uninitiated, as example b) illustrates, but if all the crucial elements fit together properly, your business plan will do its job for you.

---

i Gina Vega, "When Entrepreneurs Turn Into Managers" *(Ph.D.* diss., The Union Institute Graduate School, 1995).
ii Ichak Adizes, *Corporate Lifecycles: How and Why Corporations Grow and Die and What to Do About It".* (Upper Saddle River, NJ: Prentice Hall, 1988).
iii Webster's *Dictionary of the English Language.* (1989).

Chapter 2

———————————————➤

Road Map or Dream Catcher?

More books and articles than I can count refer to the business plan as a "road map" for your business or a "road map" to success. Where is success, anyway? I can understand a road map to Topeka or a road map to Amarillo -- I've never visited these places, but I am confident that they exist in time, space, and geography.

But success -- where is that place that a road map could guide me there? Neither your idea of success nor mine exists as a place, a specific location at the intersection of the Hard Work Highway and Lender's Lane.

No, a business plan is not a road map. A road map describes what already exists, and your plan describes what *can* be. Your plan is the expression of your entrepreneurial dream. It describes what *will* exist when you succeed. Your best-case scenario, your virtual business, thrives on paper long before it becomes a reality.

A business plan is more like an artist's conception than a road map. In it, you describe your vision, the assets and abilities that you and your team bring to the vision, and the way you intend to bring that vision to life.

Your plan is as unique as you are. When you read a plan, you should be able to see the people behind it. These are real people, with big ideas and sound ways to implement them. If you cannot see them, the plan has no life, no spirit. Without spirit, the business it represents is not likely to succeed. The plans featured in this book are full of life -- they fairly grab you by the collar and shout, "Look out. I'm coming through!"

How do you write a plan that suits your business, in your industry, at your life cycle stage, that also has spirit and personality, especially if writing has not been your strong point in the past? The key is to be natural, be yourself, and use some sense. For example, your vision **must** be written with passion, but your financials should not.

The Generic Business Plan

Your plan will be designed cafeteria-style: you put on your tray only what you like. But just as a meal of chocolate pudding is not nourishing, neither is a business plan functional if it only reflects operations (or any one element). You need a selection from each of the elements or groups: financials, marketing, management, and operations.

Element 1: Financials

Although the financials rarely appear as the first section of a business plan, we must acknowledge one truism – if the numbers don't work, the business will fail.

Making the numbers work will have different meanings according to your specific situation. At a minimum, a business plan needs to provide a balance sheet, a break-even analysis, a cash flow statement, and a 3-year income projection. (See chart in Appendix A.) If you are seeking funds, you must include a loan application and financial history or an investor prospectus. An established firm, in business for three or more years, may also include a 3-year income statement, copies of tax returns, a profit and loss statement, a history of financial reports, and selected ratios. Other, more specialized reports may be included if they satisfy specialized needs.

Element 2: Operations

This is the core of your plan. It tells the reader what you do and how you do it. Whether you provide a service, a product, or some combination of the two, this element needs to embody all the passion and excitement you can muster. If you're not a "true believer," you will find it very difficult to interest others.

"Musts" for this section are a full and complete description of the product or service, full product design information, a production plan, and the location both of the facility and of the sales areas. Results of studies of industry trends, information about production systems and goals (for example, quality assurance (QA) indicators), lists of suppliers, and the overall strategy specifying your competitive advantage may also appear.

Element 3: Marketing

The best product in the world **still** has to be sold. Your marketing plan can make or break you -- research, analysis, and access to markets will protect your product or service while you establish your sales beachhead.

Regardless of the stage of development your business is in, you will want to be sure you include three key sections in your marketing plan -- an analysis of the competition, a description of the target market, and a general marketing strategy (the way you intend to position your product). You may include within these sections information about specific promotions, pricing, the rationale for the timing of your market entry, distribution channels, and an indication of your sales areas. Some of you will also want to provide sales forecasts and related budgets, if these do not appear in your financials.

Element 4: Management

Sometimes this part of the business plan is called the organizational plan, but no matter what you call it, it is the first place investors or funding institutions will look. This is where you must establish your business' credibility if you expect to attract any outside support, debt or equity funding, or entice new talent to join your team.

An overall description of your business, an explanation of your basic management structure, a portrait of key management personnel, an indication of general staffing policies/needs, and an organization chart are critical components of this section. You will want to name the members of your Advisory Board to provide additional support for the strength and stability of your management team. For the same reason, you will include other advisors (such as attorney, CPA, consultants, etc.) and their credentials in this section as part of your support organization. Mission and organizational goals and objectives play a prominent role in this section, and should be written in plain English. In fact, avoiding jargon as much as possible will make your plan more attractive to the reader and potential supporters.

Here is where you describe the organization's legal structure, its administrative procedures, licenses required and obtained, and specific record keeping processes that add value or differentiate your business from the one next door. A third level of description would relate to international operations, anticipated effects of use of the loan proceeds (if applicable), or other unique management or administrative issues that need to be disclosed.

Element 5: Ethics

Traditionally, ethics has not had its own section in business plans, at least not in *initial* plans for businesses. However, many companies recognize that, if they do not formally articulate their ethics, the danger of inadvertent lapses increases. Nearly all industries and professional societies maintain a code of ethics, geared to the specific needs of the group in question. An extensive list of these can be found at the Online Codes of Ethics Project (http://csep.iit.edu/codes), compiled in 1999 by Center for the Study of Ethics in the Professions at Illinois Institute of Technology.

Your ethics plan should include a process for performing regular ethical audits as well as a formal Code of Ethics and, if the nature of your business warrants it, a set of procedures to ensure the ethical conduct of employees at all levels. Samples of both an Ethical Audit and a Code of Ethics appear in Appendix B.

The U.S. Department of Commerce has established a set of five areas of concern that a business is likely to want to address. These include:

1. Provision of a safe and healthy workplace.
2. Fair employment practices, including avoidance of child and forced labor and avoidance of discrimination based on race, gender, national origin or religious beliefs; and respect for the right of association and the right to organize and bargain collectively.
3. Responsible environmental protection and environmental practices.
4. Compliance with U.S. and local laws promoting good business practices, including laws prohibiting illicit payments and ensuring fair competition.
5. Maintenance, through leadership at all levels, of a corporate culture that respects free expression consistent with legitimate business concerns, and does not condone political coercion in the workplace; that encourages good corporate citizenship and makes a positive contribution to the communities in which the company operates; and where ethical conduct is recognized, valued and exemplified by all employees. [1]

Supporting Documentation

Attach copies of any documents that will enhance the way your company presents itself to others. This consists of personal resumes of key personnel, the owner's financial statement (for a start-up), copies of relevant leases, licenses, contracts, letters of reference, pre-production orders, and any credit reports that support your funding application. You may also wish to supply location studies, various financial or operational projections, demographic reports as appropriate, job descriptions, a list of capital assets if it does not appear in your financials, or any other material that will suggest your stability, engender confidence in your future, or provide appropriate disclosure.

The Order of the Plan

All plans contain certain critical elements. These elements play a more or less significant role, according to the specific use of the plan. How you label the sections of your plan is totally irrelevant, as long as you are careful to include the appropriate pieces necessary for a coherent presentation. You should assemble your plan in a way that makes sense to *you* and that serves *your* needs, while still being clear and understandable to your reader. An Executive Summary focusing on the reason you have written the plan will guide the reader through your design. If your purpose is to obtain funding, here is where you present your initial "case."

One plan in this book begins with a strategic analysis and a three-year narrative that describes goals. The financials follow, then the marketing plan and sales reports. Organizational charts and staffing plans appear at the end.[2]

Another begins with an extensive description of the company products, the organizational structure, the talent, and the philosophy that drives the business. An operational plan comes next, followed by the financial section. Goals wrap up the end.[3]

A third plan starts with marketing and distribution, followed by financials and a production plan. This plan ends with an elaborate explanation of management philosophy.[4]

The owners' individual reasons for setting up their plans the way they did will become clear as you read through them. The generic plan that follows is for a mythical company designed by a student of entrepreneurship. It includes all the sections mentioned in this chapter. I have provided this plan as an illustration of plan elements, therefore much of it will not apply to your own business.

Please remember -- the plan that follows includes virtually all components of the four elements. Your plan probably will not. The format of this plan is highly traditional; yours may differ dramatically and still be "right."

---

900 HELP ME®
January 1997
Business Plan Version 5.2
Gregory T. Simpson
President and Chief Executive Officer

1900 East 89th Street, Suite 9001E
New York, New York 19004-3576
Executive Summary

900 HELP ME is a 275 employee, New York City-based corporation which was established on January 1, 1996 to assist motorists in reaching the nearest automobile roadside assistance provider. 900 HELP ME currently offers service in all 48 continental US states.

900 HELP ME has trademarked the name AutoMedic™ to refer to our chain of automobile roadside assistance providers and we will use this term throughout the document. 900 HELP ME embraces recently developed telecommunications technology to automatically route stranded motorist's telephone calls (both wireless/cellular and traditional wire-line) to the nearest AutoMedic or local auto road-side assistance provider.

The purpose of this business plan is to secure $500,000 in additional capital to expand into Canada. The telecommunications infrastructure in Canada is currently being upgraded to support applications such as 900 HELP ME. We anticipate our largest expense to be marketing and advertising. We estimate the total cost to expand into Canada at US$500,000. 100,000 calls at the equivalent of US$5 will need to be placed to recoup the amount of the loan. If 1% of the 29.9 million automobile owners in Canada call our number one time in the first year, with a gross profit margin of $4 per call, we will have enough to pay the $500,000 loan off almost two and one half times over in the first year alone.

Letters of reference and detailed financial information and forecasts can be found in this business plan.

TABLE OF CONTENTS

I. Management
 a. Business description
 b. Management structure
 c. Key management personnel
 d. Staffing policies
 e. Organization chart
 f. Advisory board

g. Other advisors
h. Mission statement
i. Organizational goals and objectives
j. Legal structure
k. Action plan for loan proceeds

II. Operations
a. Service description
b. Service design
c. Facility locations
d. Sales areas
e. Industry trends
f. Operational Goal
g. Suppliers
h. Overall strategy

III. Marketing
a. Competitive analysis
b. Target market
c. Marketing strategy
d. Promotions
e. Pricing
f. Market entry
g. Distribution channels
h. Sales areas
i. Sales forecasts

IV. Financial Information
a. Balance sheet (including history and three year projections)
b. Income statement (including history and three year projections)
c. Statement of cash flows
d. Break-even analysis
e. Loan application
f. Letters of reference/ Summary resumes

V. Ethics
a. Business Principles
b. Code of Conduct
c. Procedure for Ethical Audit

I. MANAGEMENT

a. Business description:

900 HELP ME is a business which was established on January 1, 1996 to enable motorists to reach the nearest automobile roadside assistance provider anytime. As previously mentioned, 900 HELP ME has trademarked the name AutoMedic to refer to our automobile roadside assistance branch locations.

900 HELP ME utilizes a technology which automatically routes telephone calls (both wireless/cellular and traditional wire-line) to the nearest AutoMedic or the nearest local auto road-side assistance provider.

Initially 900 HELP ME simply brought stranded motorists and the closest auto road-side assistance providers together on the phone when distressed motorists solicited road-side assistance. 900 HELP ME compiled the best practices, procedures, and methods used by the most successful auto road-side assistance provider from around the globe. This information was then used to build our chain of 900 HELP ME AutoMedic.

Our customers are distressed motorists in need of assistance. This group consists of anyone of legal driving age, located in the US who needs assistance and who has access to a telephone. Distressed drivers are motivated to dial our number because we guarantee that we will connect them with the closest AutoMedic or auto road-side assistance provider. Of course, the service must also be offered at an affordable price (pre-approved by 900 HELP ME).

900 HELP ME was founded by Gregory T. Simpson, who conceived this company when his car broke down while he was traveling out of town. He was sitting in his car on the side of the road with his cellular phone in his hand ready to dial for help, but he didn't know whom to call. He thought, "Wouldn't it be great if there was a nationally accessible phone number that connected people with the closest service station." While waiting for the tow truck to arrive, Greg called a few of his business associates and asked them what they thought of his idea. They all agreed that it was a winner, and when Greg returned home he started the wheels in motion. Greg was initially involved in this

1994 Sales by Product Category

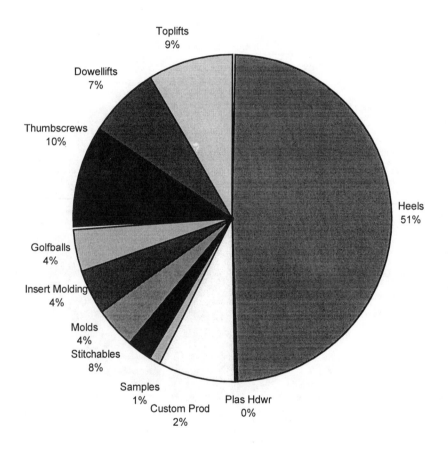

A Passion for Planning

1995 Sales by Product Category

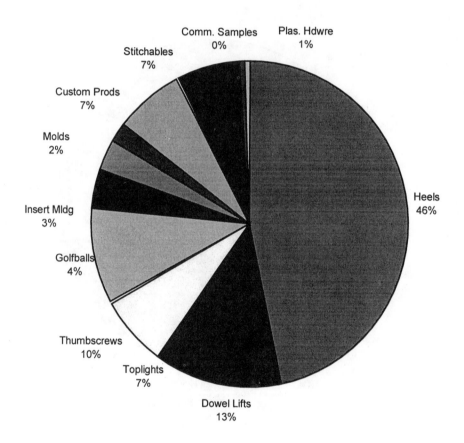

PLASTECHS, INC.
Sales Analysis by Customer

Customer Code	Budget 1994	Actual 1994	Budget 1995
001	40,200	61,863	54,673
002	22,100	11,499	10,359
003	15,508	3,774	
004	199,934	198,063	197,640
005	19,193	27,958	24,654
006	94,591	129,847	296,025
007	130,687	125,617	132,472
008	742,228	682,187	517,735
009	69,401	110,936	119,981
010	17,970	30,924	27,530
011	20,150	30,518	34,097
012	4,000	9,234	6,714
013	414,361	361,010	363,970
014	383,839	244,090	248,098
015	10,000	11,900	7,673
016	117,600	56,240	49,108
017	25,000	44,983	47,765
018	27,500	41,862	21,149
019	7,138	2,464	
020	719,731	939,417	919,334
021	14,000	26,760	52,944
022	32,000	100,282	107,999
023	11,000	5,060	7,913
024	205,000	157,952	189,525
025	75,000	153,671	147,515
026	177,096	171,930	180,974
027	34,941	42,140	40,678
028	379,563	386,780	374,395
029	18,000	44,364	42,729
030	120,000	46,471	0
031	17,000	31,624	36,399
032	70,000	21,497	13,428
033	165,676	152,405	197,229

034	39,714	22,666	22,928
035	257,150	241,582	240,072
036	47,117	47,750	46,034
037	99,388	108,219	104,289
038	35,165	28,978	23,832
039	31,530	66,905	58,809
040	9,000	11,371	13,907
041	71,786	34,258	32,872
042	54,793	27,487	8,547
043	45,648	24,195	37,949
044	15,114	2,405	
045		8,000	
046		27,790	41,999
047		7,817	4,796
048		10,391	14,387
049		13,770	
050		13,200	16,833
051		25,864	21,448
052		10,916	364,135
053		18,609	33,570
054		11,857	11,510
055		10,357	
Miscellaneous	623,550	233,345	310,634
TOTAL	**5,727560**	**5,473,054**	**5,879,256**

In examining the "Sales by Product Category" charts, we see a decrease in sales of toplifts from 1994 to 1995, as well as a 5% decrease in sales of heels. Yet, Plastechs states a series of sales objectives that focus on gaining market share in the domestic and foreign footwear industry, as well as pursuing toplift business in dance shoes. What is the purpose of this focus when they have increased their production of custom products over the same time period by 5% and intend to have 50% of revenue derived from non-traditional product by year end of 1995?

It's easy to slip into this kind of inconsistent planning if you have not selected a clear strategy to pursue at the growth stage. When we set a strategy, we need to consider our objectives alongside production history and a realistic expectation of future production needs based on sales analysis by customer (as provided above). This sales analysis seems to clarify the changing market for Plastechs' products from footwear to alternative products, and may suggest that some of their objectives should be realigned.

Lacey concurs that productivity initiatives must be aligned with strategy even when they do not follow from it. In other words, some productivity initiatives will directly support a firm's chosen strategy; others make sense doing over a number of several strategies. Yet, some may contradict a firm's strategic direction. For example, Plastechs' objective to reduce overtime would support a strategy that seeks to compete on price. The objective to monitor the cost and value of employee benefits would make sense despite the strategy chosen, and is thus well aligned. But if a strategy of superior service through maximum flexibility was chosen, then an initiative to reduce overtime could become a hindrance.

The job for Plastechs' management is to choose a strategic direction, then decide which productivity gains are most important in following that direction. To put this a different way, productivity initiatives are the internal plans that help enable the firm's external strategic direction, but many of these initiatives require more specificity. Rather than a sales objective to "continue to gain market share in the footwear industry," one that commits to increase share from 10% to 12% is more meaningful. Not all objectives must be put in quantitative terms, but all must include built-in performance measures such as a due dates. And, each objective must support the strategic direction, or productivity gains, or both. For example, pursuing telemarketing as a sales tool does not seem to support either, since Plastechs is not a mass market retailer. Objectives that do not support strategy or productivity -- directly or indirectly -- must be dropped.

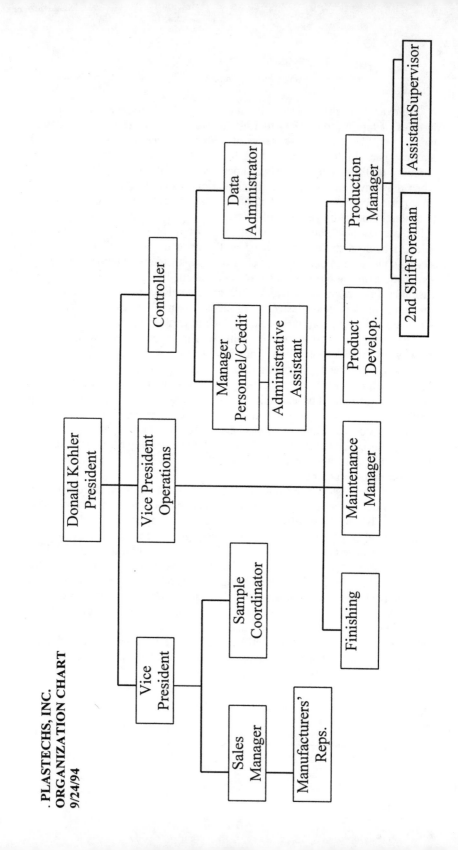

. PLASTECHS, INC.
ORGANIZATION CHART
9/24/94

ORGANIZATION CHART
9/29/95

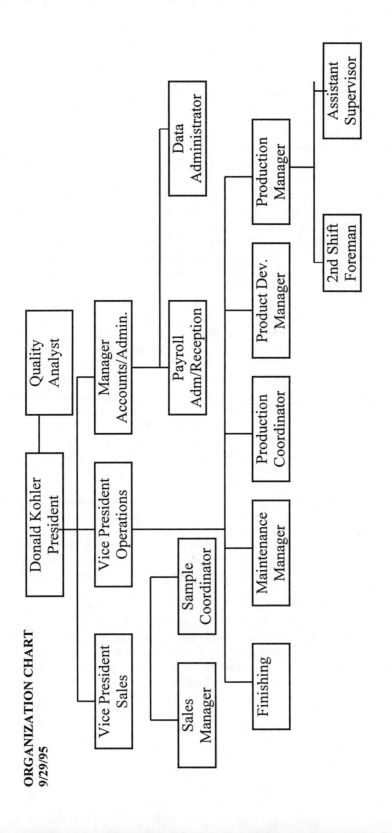

As a manufacturer functions within the growth cycle, we can see from Plastechs' organization charts that there is no real need for additional organizational complexity, just for additional clarity. In fact, the development of Plastechs' organization charts indicates some simplifications, such as the removal of manufacturer's reps from their reporting relationship to the sales manager. The addition of the quality analyst and a production coordinator can be explained by the new focus on quality, which is directly related to improved production methods. There has been some "correction" in task assignment, by reassigning payroll and accounts administration to a "manager" and removing them from the "controller." The titles are not important in themselves, but it appears that Donald Kohler has managed to combine several functions and effectively eliminate the need for a full time high salary position. This change is in line with Plastechs' stated goal of decentralizing responsibility and authority through the empowerment of employees. If this kind of change is your strategy as well, you will want to make sure that the elimination of a position will not put you at risk of a weakened management structure.

As Lacey suggests, the management team needs to come up to speed on industry "best practices." Best practices refers to a set of proven approaches that are likely to have positive results. They have, through trial, error, and significant testing, been shown to work better than other current approaches. Some of the objectives indicate that Plastechs has problems that have plagued other firms for decades, but where much progress has been made through best practices. To cite a specific example, several initiatives mention increasing throughput, improving customer promises, or improving factory scheduling. The industry best practice that addresses these issues is a materials management methodology called manufacturing resource planning, or MRP II for short. Plastechs should thus make implementing a computer-based MRP II system a key objective. In another case, an objective seeks to spend 2% of payroll for training. In the United States, benchmarking shows that firms spend an average of 1.4% of <u>revenue</u> on training, much more than 2% of payroll. And the best firms spend even more.

Many objectives would be better expressed as creating "competencies." Competencies are the skills an organization creates to achieve strategic and productivity goals. For example, a training objective to "promote cross training of all personnel to enhance flexibility" would be expressed as "create a cross-trained workforce." The cross-trained workforce is the competence that Plastechs creates to become more productive.

Epilogue

A plan that looks scattershot on its face may, in fact, have served the needs of the business at the time it was written. This innovative plan brought Plastechs back from the brink of disaster when their traditional markets disappeared. Donald Kohler refers to himself as "the last iceman," because he can identify only one real competitor remaining in the industry. But because being the last iceman was never his goal, he has led his team in brainstorming "crazy" (his own description) ideas and firing a lot of buckshot.

The major strategic decision they made was to not permit any customer to account for more than 10 percent of their business, having learned their uncomfortable lesson with the departure of the shoe industry. They discovered that, since the molding machines don't know what they're making, it makes no difference what they make. This opened the door to a great many lucrative opportunities. For example, Plastechs took the screw from a heel lift and transformed it into a screw for a computer cable at a 600 percent increase in profit.

They work closely with inventors, developing prototypes and often becoming the sole producers of specialized products. They are always on the lookout for the next opportunity, the new market, the idiosyncratic quirk that will put them ahead of the crowd. And they have succeeded. Not only has Plastechs, Inc. survived, it has thrived and continues to grow today.

If your manufacturing company is trying to enter the growth stage, what can you do to ease the passage? Plastechs, Inc. teaches us two important lessons:

1. We need to think "outside the box." If your machinery can weave broadloom for carpets, can it also weave nylon for artificial grass? If your machinists can tool dies, can they also make the inserts for metal files? Is the technology similar for producing baby bottles and toner cartridges?

2. As a business "grows up," it may need to depersonalize ownership and introduce ways to push control down to the lowest possible level. Plastechs does this through a Gain Share program, a phantom stock plan, a personnel training and cross/training program, and management succession planning. How you do this for your own business is strictly dependent on your personal style, however, you must select a way to transfer some operations responsibilities from yourself to your staff in order to preserve your energies for strategic planning and design.

Chapter 5

---------------------→

Problems and Opportunities

Maturity brings with it its own set of problems and new opportunities. Companies age in many of the same ways that people age. People who keep active tend to age more gracefully than those who don't budge from the easy chair, and businesses that continue to adapt remain more flexible and able to change as the need arises or the opportunity presents itself. Our first grey hair or wrinkle surprises us, and our reaction to these changes signals the likelihood that we will make a comfortable and successful transition to a new stage of development. The business equivalent of signs like wrinkles and grey hair may include a certain reluctance to invest in new technology, an unwillingness to engage in conflict, and a slowdown of Research & Development activity.

Once again, your business plan can help you through this crisis of development. If you are prepared to re-evaluate your purpose, possibly restructure your company, and investigate new possibilities in related fields, even a mature company in a mature industry can continue to grow and thrive. Special Products, Inc. is an excellent example of this process. It has reinvented itself for the third time, and sales have continued to grow, profitability has increased, and several new jobs have been created.

Case Example #3 - Special Products, Inc.

Coupled with the maturity issue of reinvention, a challenge that is frequently overlooked by small businesses, both in a manufacturing and in a service environment, is how to handle risk-taking in a litigious environment. A society that tends to respond to problems with immediate and costly legal action often limits creativity in manufacturers and encourages them to move their facilities to a "friendlier" location.

Special Products, Inc. is a mature company that manufactures adaptive equipment for people with various disabilities, as well as athletic protective gear and devices. These products lend themselves to consumer complaints which lead to lawsuits and other legal entanglements that, whether justified or not, pull resources away from basic operations. It takes a special kind of courage and commitment to keep your business in the United States rather than moving towards off-shore manufacturing to avoid the legal turmoil. Special Products has made that commitment, and that philosophy of U.S. production guides their plans for growth and development.

At the time of the following plan's writing, their financial health was poor, with a corporate net worth just over $250,000 and pretax earnings under $100,000. Other similar businesses were relocating, product liability insurance had skyrocketed from $2500 annually to $1000 weekly, and the product market had shifted from institutional to individual, making each sale more costly and less profitable.

When your business provides you with what Maria Jacobs, President of Special Products, Inc. calls the "dark nights of the soul," these are the questions that you need to ask:

- What is my *real* business?
- Is it worth the continuing effort to stay on the same track?
- Should I rethink my product, my market, my core competencies, my human resources?
- Should I be cutting costs and narrowing my vision or investing, expanding, and refocusing?
- And, do I have the right people in place to implement my plan?

We will look at the answers to these questions for Special Products, and how you might answer the same questions in your business.

Special Products' business plan has an appropriate focus on its value added processes, definition and redefinition of the core business, and sales budgets and processes. However, despite being a mature company, they have written their plan in the area of operations as if they were a start-up. This is partly the result of a corporate refocus that forces them to reassess their positioning in all areas, and partly the result of rocky transitions, which could be described as over control or micro-management. Above all, we can learn from Special Products that business plans (and businesses) are not easily pigeon-holed; rarely is there a perfect fit between the model and the reality.

Special Products, Inc.

STATEMENT OF PURPOSE
AND
BUSINESS PLAN

Update #6 - 1994

Statement of Purpose

Special Products, Inc. is formed for the purpose of the invention and the creation of specialty equipment that can be used to encourage participation in many of life's activities. This equipment is used by the physically and mentally challenged, as well as athletes meeting individual challenges. Our objectives will be met by our concentration of energies into unique and innovative ways to reach the markets that we serve. By always being responsive to the needs of our end users, and listening to them, we will produce only top quality goods and services.

To be an equal opportunity employer, and to provide our employees with excellent working conditions and salaries substantial enough to afford them to be able to choose the lifestyle that they desire are also goals of this company. We will be contributing to our community, state and country, as we strive to be an example of successful corporate culture.

Introduction

Our business plan is divided into five sections, which describe our operations in each of these areas:

Physical Plant
Financial
Human Resources
Production
Sales and Marketing

We continually update our plan as significant changes occur in our history. We want to provide a "snapshot" of our business that is both timely and accurate. Now that we are nearing our twenty-fifth year in business, we know and understand the importance of our mission statement and goals. By keeping our business plan current, we not only can build future strategies, we also have an historical record of our past milestones and achievements for the archival records.

Each of these five areas are weighted equally, as they are synergetic parts of our whole business. We recognize the contributions of all of our past employees, and look forward to the future with confidence, based on the multi-talented individuals who are part of our ever evolving team.

Company History

Founded in 1968 for the manufacture of protective headgear for wrestlers, Special Products was owned and managed by two partners. Max Oberson was the design engineer, who was formerly an instructor at the University of Wisconsin School of Architecture and Design, and Courtland Pitt who was the materials technologist, who ran another business at the time. Both were University of Wisconsin wrestling alumni, and pooled their knowledge of the sports field to begin their business. Together, they expanded the company for $25,000 in yearly sales to $500,000 within ten years. Oberson then bought out Pitt and became sole owner. A key employee was promoted to President and General Manager, allowing Oberson to expand his research and development into other types of protective headgear. This led to our Special Needs line of equipment specifically designed for persons with mental and/or physical disabilities. For the next few years, various styles of headgear and swimming aids were marketed for both children and adults. Innovative techniques were used, and we received Wisconsin New Product of the Year Awards not once, but twice.

In 1983, Maria Jacobs joined Special Products. By concentrating her efforts on the fledgling Special Needs line through sales efforts and marketing strategy, this new area grew from $150,000 annually to $1,200,000 within eight years. Our staff grew from five employees to twenty-seven full time employees. During this same time period, the athletic/wrestling sales grew to $800,000. We now manufacture nearly 80% of all the high school and collegiate wrestling helmets used in the United States. There is much cross-fertilization between these two seemingly different product lines in both manufacturing systems and materials technology. In designing both athletic equipment and equipment for the disabled, there are similar issues to be addressed. Protection against unintentional contact, comfort for the user, proper fit, attractive, durable, and reasonably priced all are factors that must be considered.

Because of our uniqueness and expertise in this field, in 1983 and 1984, Oberson worked as the Technology Consultant for two projects through the Madison County Intermediate School District which involved Wheelchair/Classroom Chair Headrest Development. Many new products were brought to market as a result of that study and were featured in a new full color catalog published in 1986. This new classification of positioning equipment broadened our customer base immensely.

In 1983 we had two durable medical equipment dealers, and currently we have over 2,000 covering every state in the union and in some foreign countries. Our Retail Customer List has grown from 500 to 15,000 during that same time period. This growth necessitated computerizing our database in 1985. This system is now being replaced and upgraded as we outgrew its capacity.

In 1988, Jacobs bought Special Products and is now the sole shareholder and Oberson is retained under contract as a consultant for research and design projects. In 1989, we moved to a bigger and better facility to enhance our growth opportunities.

We have never lost sight of our original objective, to deliver top quality equipment to our marketplace in a timely and efficient manner and to continually be responsive to their needs. By doing that, we have gained a reputation as "the problem solvers" in our industry. People bring us all kind of requests for specialized equipment that cannot be found. We either source it or manufacture it to meet their specifications. In 1986, we opened a new department in the company because of these requests. It grew from one part time employee to 3 and a half people currently. This unique and innovative department builds orders on a "one to one" basis. Anything from a customer helmet to a custom wheelchair system is constructed from measurements, casts, patterns or diagrams submitted by medical professionals. To our knowledge, we are the only company in our field to offer such specialized services.

Our four color catalog is now over 110 pages long, and is written in three languages, English, French, and Spanish -- a real milestone in our development. This comprehensive catalog is also used by many professors in their physical therapy and occupational therapy classes as a guide for adaptive equipment usage.

Physical Plant

With the acquisition of new plant facilities in 1989, our office and production space tripled, allowing us to expand both our wrestling/athletic operations and our Special Needs equipment line. We are now located 1/2 mile off of I-94 on the Western edge of Monona. As part of our acquisition, we purchased a second building with the 10.5 acre parcel of land for investment purposes. It is a commercial warehouse/office/light assembly building, which was fully leased at the time of purchase. As our business grows, we plan on using this second building for our own expansion. The tenant leases have staggered lease ending dates, so that our moves will occur with minimal disruption. The 24,000 square foot building now has 7 tenants, and with one lease expiring now, we have 3,000 square feet for our use.

We have physically separated the two divisions of our operations as they no longer share equipment or personnel. The wrestling/athletic manufacturing has moved into this other building and now occupies a 3,000 square foot area, which enabled us to expand the Special Needs area. The Customs Department now moved into that space as we really needed more space due to the increased number of orders that they must process. As we grow more, other departments can be relocated at this second building, which is only 100 yards away. The next planned phase will be to move the finished goods and Shipping/Receiving Department, which would result in 2,000 more square feet of manufacturing space.

In addition to the full athletic/manufacturing end of the business being relocated into this second building, we also are going to install the offices for our new retail sales company to be called Complete Adaptive and Athletic Equipment, Inc. From that office, we will be selling various athletic equipment, including wrestling headgear which will be purchased from PL Forest for resale. The other phase of this double pronged business will be our new wheelchair seating department. A customer casting chair will be installed here. We will be doing customer wheelchair fittings and handling durable medical equipment sales to the general public. This dual use of space will continue until sales increase to the point that additional space will needed.

Situated on the 10.5 acres in Carr Township, we also have an option to build in the future, or even to sell off a parcel of land if we choose to do so. This enables us to remain flexible and respond to our growth requirements in an efficient and reasonable manner.

Special Products, Inc. is keenly aware of its position as market leader and of its commitment to its specialized customer base. Once again, as we saw in the previous case of a manufacturing company in the growth phase, the need for corporate direction stirs the sleeping giant, strategy. There are three generic strategies that a company can follow: they can focus on the uniqueness of their product (product differentiation); they can serve a particular market niche (customer focus); or they can be the least expensive comparable provider of product or service (cost leadership). It matters very little which strategy a company selects. What does matter is that they *must* select one in order to determine where to allocate the bulk of their resources most effectively.

Special Products describes a history of change and reinvention that is customer-driven. That is, they have traditionally responded to the needs of their customers and have adapted their own product to meet those needs. In fact, they have developed a proprietary technology that permits them to make the adaptations and individualized products that they sell. They have successfully implemented the lesson we gleaned from Plastechs -- thinking outside the box made it clear to them that equipment that protects athletes from accidental injury can be adapted to protect people with disabilities from similar injuries. They have thus developed a hybrid strategy, one that focuses both on customer and on product. The primacy of the Research and Development division has resulted in the purchase of new facilities which will ultimately serve for the planned expansion of operations for Special Products. However, as the next plan section demonstrates, the purchase of real estate may not be in the best interest of the company at the present time.

Gayle Porter, member of the faculty of the School of Business at Rutgers University, comments, "The history portion of the business plan relates innovation and responsiveness, as Special Products, Inc. has created many successful products, a new department for customization, their "special needs" line, and they have become known as "the problem solvers." Retaining Oberson as a consultant for R&D should help maintain the established quality standards. It seems that this company has identified a cluster of product offerings in which they excel by offering innovative and specialized products and services. In fact they may be setting the standard for others who would enter these markets. The company history supports they have been successful in pursuing their objectives related to quality, innovation, and customer focus.

Nonetheless, under Physical Plant, I was surprised to see the land and building purchase for investment purposes. It does offer them flexibility for future growth. The downside is that it puts them in the property management business in the meantime. Perhaps this organization is more comfortable with that situation, because the president's background is property management, and others have somewhat related experience in apartment and hotel management. (*You will see evidence of this in the Human Resources section of the plan.*) Still, someone is investing time and energy in this activity rather than the real business of the company. Many organizations in the past decade have trimmed down to stay competitive. One way they have done so is by retaining only their primary business activity, those things they do best, and eliminating other distractions. Special Products seems to be moving the other way, which could become a threat to the very growth they are preparing for.

There is also a danger that having the space available might result in their comfortably expanding into it before they feel any real growing pains. The innovative spirit they apply in product design might also serve them well in finding more efficient processes and plant layouts, if they have need to explore those options. With the easy availability of space, and incremental opportunities to expand, they may prematurely assume fixed costs that otherwise would be delayed until absolutely necessary. These are concerns are not predictive of what will happen, only cautions of what could happen.

Financial

Historically, we have continually and steadily maintained a growth rate of over 10% per year for the last 5 years. Revenue has all been reinvested back into the company, with no dividends being taken back by the owner. We always have been a self-funded company and while this has its advantages in many ways, it also has limited our rate of growth to what we can immediately pay for in terms of research and development of new products.

The asset side of our balance sheet shows good cash flow and solid receivables. In the last few years, our write off for bad debt has been around 1%. By maintaining this tight a control on our billings, we can forecast our cash flow expectations accurately. The liabilities side of our balance sheet reflects the recent purchase of Special Products by Jacobs, with a consulting contract for ten years being extended to Oberson. There is also a non-compete agreement which runs concurrently with that contract.

Our real estate is currently on land contract which has a balloon payment in 1998. As the interest rates get more favorable, the plan is to convert to a mortgage and pay off our land contract holder. With a rate of 1% over prime, floating and adjustable quarterly, we still benefit as the interest rates drop.

With the addition of our Chief Financial Officer, Ansel Peterson who came aboard in 1987, our accounting functions have been upgraded and improved. Monthly meetings are held with the Board of Directors to discuss each financial statement and analyze the figures.

Any expenses running over the budgeted figures are closely scrutinized to determine the reason and decide on a course of action. Purchasing is controlled through this department as well. All purchase orders are approved by the company President. The Sales Manager gives weekly reports to the CFO with breakdowns by dealer, non-dealer and model numbers of equipment sold. Annual figures are broken down geographically and are based from accounting to the marketing department for their analysis.

Human Resources

A company can only be as strong as its employees make it. We plan to grow and add staff as we have in the past -- with a strong belief that a variety of skill levels, a variety of personalities, and a variety of ethnic diversity is the key to success. Our people are strong because of their differences more so than their similarities. Corporate culture can stagnate by cloning a staff in management's image.

Because of our nurturing atmosphere, we encourage people to express their views and ideas about their working environment. In this way, many changes and improvements were initiated that otherwise may never have been thought of. A highly successful Profit Sharing Plan has been in place since 1978, and has been funded every year since then. Contributions have been averaging over 10%, and many of our staff members are now fully vested. They have been able to buy homes, and handled financial emergencies because of their participation in this plan.

We proudly participate in a local vocational training program for students with multiple handicaps. They come each semester as part of the school curriculum and learn the proper ways to interact in a work setting. There are non-ambulatory, non-verbal and severely handicapped students who otherwise may not get a chance to experience "going to work." Each year at our annual full staff meeting, we honor them with Certificates of Completion, and a remembrance from Special Products.

Growing from a staff of 2 to 27, we believe in promoting from within, and most of our current managers started in production many years ago. One of the benefits of that philosophy is that we do not have an "us and them" mentality. We respect and admire each member of our staff, realizing that we have synergetic relationships, and that is one of the contributing factors to our success. Salaries are based on four basic criteria: teamwork, quality of output, individual goal attainment and corporate profit.

Each of our management positions is filled by high caliber persons who are aware of their professionalism and responsibilities. in the future we know that we will attract more people like this who want to enhance their careers at Special Products.

Maria Jacobs, President
Owner of Special Products since 1988. Began as General Manager and Director of Operations in 1983 with five employees, and has steadily broadened the scope and depth of Special's activities. Under her leadership, there has been a steady growth rate averaging over 10% annually. By actively presenting at in-services, symposiums, and at sales outlets, she has showcased products, successfully marketing them to medical professionals from all over the world. Previously was Vice-President and General Manager of a property management corporation based in the Southeast Wisconsin area, at which she specialized in the renovation of distressed commercial properties then participated in their resale. Also was responsible for hotel management, multi-family units, and restaurant management as these properties came into the portfolio.

Ansel Peterson, Vice-President
Joined the management team in 1987, and brought a strong financial background to Special. As the Chief Financial Officer, he has successfully forecasted growth and controlled the resulting expenses. Sets all budgets, both yearly and for our five year plan. With a close control of receivables he has kept bad debt write-offs to under 2% each of the last three years. As both Controller and General Manager of a large hotel/restaurant operation in Oklahoma, his previous positions included both financial and human resources capabilities. As an active hands on manager, he directed

the sales operation which recruited business which put his property at the top of the chain.

Patricia Conway, Director of Sales and Marketing

Since 1986, when she joined Special as the Director of Sales, she has been responsible for training the sales staff, as well as coordinating the specialty department of customized equipment. Dealing with medical experts from all over the country, she has established a reputation as an expert in this field. Customers rely on her input to place orders that will meet their needs. Customer relations always come first and many new orders are generated because of this priority. Her previous position in apartment management required a high level of organization and she was instrumental in the planning and implementation of many new information systems. She contributed to the successful growth of this company as they continually expanded in their marketplace.

Peter Mann, Engineer

Job responsibilities, which he assumed in 1985, include physical plant, manufacturing science, materials science, and research and development. He bridges the R & D prototype stage into the production stage of our products, determining tooling requirements or outsourced services. By integrating the most effective systems for commercialization and marketing of our equipment, he contributes directly to the sales team. He also adds design touches for our final product presentations, and also design our exhibit and traveling displays. In his former management job, he created models and prototypes for agribusiness.

Steve Andrews, Rehabilitation Equipment Technician

With nearly 15 years of experience in seating the disabled, he has established himself as an expert in the Southeast Wisconsin area. Working with many severely disabled clients, he has been implemental in designing many customer seating systems. Opening up a customer seating department in his former place of employment resulted in the creation of many new job positions, and increased services to the handicapped community. He was directly responsible for creating sales of over one million dollars within a three year period. Here at Special since 1991, we have already seen his contribution to the sales team, as he calls on our dealers of medical equipment and the many schools and facilities that we now can service.

A particularly interesting facet of this business plan revolves around the language and style of presentation. The narrative, "chatty" format of this plan represents confidence and openness of approach. Maria Jacobs is not hiding any dark secrets from us; we know the main players in this corporate drama and we can relate to them on an individual basis. Because of this, our sympathies are aroused and we wish them great success. It is valuable to create this sense of personal connection when writing a plan for a mature company, especially if you are in the process of constant reinvention.

Consistency between the "business" of business and the "process" of business (the relationship among finances, production, and human resources issues) is another cornerstone of long-term survivability. We saw it in Tom's of Maine (start-up), and we see it here as well. A company's success will depend, not in small part, on the way employees are treated and on the amount of consideration for their well-being that is provided by owners or managers. The discussion of a profit sharing plan (in place for more than 20 years), corporate commitment to community responsibility, and promotion from within, all speak to this consistency.

However, there are some rumblings of trouble in paradise. As Dr. Porter notes, "Serving as technology consultants for the school district shows some community involvement. However, there is not much in the history describing specific efforts to define and develop corporate culture, nor information about employees. In short, the history reflects congruence with the purpose of the company, and it directly addresses some, but not all, of the supporting objectives.

The coverage of Human Resources echoes the quality theme by including that as one of four criteria for salary determination. Statements in this section express that employees are valued in the organization, for example, encouraging people to express their views and promoting from within. Unfortunately, no detail is provided as to how these things are done. I would be particularly interested in how they balance rewarding both teamwork and individual goal attainment, and how they work to achieve the diversity they espouse.

The detailed coverage in this section is devoted to profiles of five key employees. After reading about these individuals, I felt I knew the company better, although it does not tell me much about the functional role of the Human Resource group in the same way the other functions described their business activity. Are there no proactive initiatives related to the objectives referencing employees? In general, I would say that HR is not out of step with the purpose and objectives of this organization, but I suspect they have not yet stepped up to being valued on par with the other functional specialties. There is some difference between valuing the people of the organization and valuing the Human Resource function, but they are closely aligned and this is a part of the organization's culture.

Looking at the Finance coverage, I had some additional concerns about the corporate culture that currently exists and their continuing growth pattern. Not only is there close scrutiny of any items over budget, but also the board of directors reviews and analyzes each financial statement once a month. The company president approves all purchase orders. Extensive weekly reports from the Sales Managers go to the CFO, then annual figures pass from finance back to marketing for analysis.

My feeling in reading this is that I'm supposed to be impressed with the tight controls and extensive record keeping. My personal reaction is that stressing flexibility on the customer side and clamping down so very tightly on the financial/administrative side is likely to cause problems as they continue to grow. This handful of people at the top seem to personally monitor business at the transaction level. Now may be the time to begin moving some of these activities down the organization, while the group is still small enough to do so as a gradual transition. They also admit that the policy of being self-funded has limited growth. They may need a more strategic look at their desired future growth rate and what internal and external supports that targeted rate will require."

Production

With steady increases in our unit volume that we normally experience, it is necessary to continually evaluate the most cost effective way to produce each product in each size and style. As both our raw materials and tooling needs are unique, it is important for us to strive for creative engineering solutions.

We are currently using a customized version of "Just in Time" systems management for both raw materials and finished goods. This will be more finely tuned and actually expanded upon to allow for our customers' more knowledgeable buying habits. They are now requiring more options, colors, sizes and styles of equipment and we must be responsible to this trend.

With this in mind, we have applied to the State of Wisconsin, Wisconsin Business Strategies 2000 program running under the Department of Commerce. Their business analysis would really be helpful at this critical time of our growth. Contacts that we would meet through this program would be the top experts in their fields.

Current tooling is always being checked for excessive wear and/or needed repair. We have replacement tooling in the budget each year. As the volume of sales increases for an item, engineering analyzes what ways would be most effective for producing it. Injection molding, drape forming, clicker cutter dies, vacuum forming, or compression molding are just some of the considerations for us in making those decisions.

Each staff member rotates in and out of job areas, so that one person does not have to do just one job all the time. This way everyone is responsible for quality too, which we found eliminated the need for a separate quality control department.

In the Special Needs line, our clientele is unique. This population accounts for more than 1% of the population, but with 99% of the variations, rendering anthropometrical standards invalid. Because of these variances, we have very few products which could ever sell over 5,000 units annually. The nature of these productions will always remain low volume and with many customizations necessary for the client.

In the wrestling/athletic side of our production, our volume of units produced rises dramatically. With over 50,000 wrestlers alone entering programs at the high school and collegiate level, our total number of units sold averages over 140,000 annually. Here, injection molding is nearly always the preferred method of producing wrestling helmets. We typically do two full years of market testing hand cut prototype models of headgear before committing to cut any steel. This way, we work out the bugs and minor changes ahead of time.

Our staff assembles the parts using fastening machines, snap machines and hot stamping equipment. A lot of manual dexterity is required, as the assembly is quick and constant. Every person on staff can do every job, so we have a lot of flexibility built into this operation.

The injection molding operation that we use is located 16 miles away from our plant, making "just in time" daily deliveries for our production requirements. We now represent over 50% of their business, with that percentage increasing annually. In the future, the sole stockholder of that company has indicated a willingness to sell his business to us. This merger of talent and molding capabilities would fit nicely into our overall plan. We have had a mutually rewarding business relationship which goes back twenty years to when his father owned the company, so there is respect on both sides, which would make that buy-out a win-win situation.

One of our future goals is to set up a system for automatic packaging. We could see as many as 200,000 headgear going out of our operation within the next couple of years, and manually packaging that number would be cost prohibitive. We are working with our customer, PL Forest Athletic, Inc. as to what their packaging preferences would be.

Other athletic equipment will round out our line, and we foresee soccer helmets and other protective equipment as our next major production goal. We have already completed one year of field testing and are ready to commit to the manufacture of this equipment, with distributors in a nationwide basis.

Sales & Marketing

With the addition of a new sales person last year, we are fully staffed to handle all the necessary functions of sales. Orders are generated from the mail, telephone calls and faxes. We have two price lists, one is Retail for our non dealer customers, such as individuals, regional centers for the mentally handicapped, and the other is our Dealer Price List for durable medical equipment vendors. Our Customer Data Base now has 20,000 customers and of that 2,000 are dealers. These dealers generate approximately 50% of our orders.

Customer orders must be submitted to the sales manager for approval prior to being sent to production. This insures proper costing and that we have all the information necessary to build the items, i.e. proper measurements, colors, etc.

In addition to inside sales just described, we also have outside sales which are handled by our same salespeople. We go into facilities, dealerships and hospitals to show our equipment. These in-services are beneficial because our line of products are unique, and the caregivers and medical staff must be able to ask questions and "touch and feel." Every time that we attend a meetings, symposium or exhibit at a show, we combine that activity with outside sales calls in that area of the country. We strive to achieve a mix of current customers, cold calls and both dealer and non-dealer sales. This has proven to be a cost effective and efficient means to service our customers.

Because our sales mix has highly specialized types of equipment which require a high degree of customization, we choose to have direct contact with the end users of such equipment. This is one of the reasons why we do not use sales representatives. This is also one of the reasons that we sell directly to the general public in addition to our dealer network. A growing and inventive company such as our needs to be "in the trenches" in order to refine and develop products. We listen to our customers and use their input to help determine our product offerings.

Our market penetration is plotted and analyzed, with many different plans for implementing stronger sales for those areas in which we want to have extensive coverage. The marketing department typically presents budgets at the beginning of each year. We use a combination of journal advertising, new product releases, press releases, newsletter inserts and exhibits at seminars to reach our customers. Additionally, we prepare at least one mailing per year to our full customer base. Catalogs are mailed by request and are free of charge. Our catalogs are often requested by professors for use by their students. The average number mailed per year is over 6,000.

We also publish a yearly calendar, which is now a tradition for us, that features our products in typical living situations. We have different artists do the calendar pictures and we also have a very complete listing of meetings and symposiums that is of great use to the professional in our field. To our knowledge, we are the only company that combines this information from many different but related fields (i.e. physical therapy, orthotics, prosthetics, occupational therapy, rehabilitation medicine, etc.) Normal distribution is between 25,000 and 30,000.

Our budget is weighted toward exhibiting at both regional and national shows. We always try to tie in any new products to be released at this type of show, as it usually creates a sensation. Many of the presenters tie in our products in their presentations, such as our Hensinger Head Support and Modular Chest Support being recommended in a lecture on transportation of the handicapped.

We also supply notes and pictures for authors who are writing on some facet of mobility recreation or positioning. We are referenced in numerous books and journal articles which reflects favorable not only on sales, but also draws many research and development opportunities to us from around the world.

SPECIAL PRODUCTS, INC.
STATEMENT OF INCOME AND RETAINED EARNINGS
YEARS ENDED DECEMBER 31, 1994 AND 1993

	1994	**1993**
NET SALES	$2,092,674	$2,034,481
COST OF GOODS SOLD	1,046,781	1,032,961
Gross Margin	1,045,893	1,001,520
OPERATING EXPENSES		
General and administrative (Note 2)	713,944	703,252
Selling	241,669	212,290
Total operating expenses	955,613	915,542
INCOME FROM OPERATIONS	90,280	85,978
OTHER INCOME (EXPENSE)		
Interest Income (Note 8)	20,093	17,694
Interest Expense (Note 8)	(53,884)	(51,868)
Other, net		420
Total other income (expense) - net	(33,791)	(33,754)
INCOME BEFORE PROVISION FOR FEDERAL INCOME TAXES	56,489	52,224
PROVISION FOR FEDERAL INCOME TAXES (Note 6)	14,304	9,912
NET INCOME	42,185	42,312
RETAINED EARNINGS - BEGINNING OF YEAR	213,525	171,213
RETAINED EARNINGS - END OF YEAR	$ 255,710	$ 213,525

[Notes to financial statements and Independent Accountants'
Compilation Report not included here]

SPECIAL PRODUCTS, INC.

STATEMENT OF CASH FLOWS
YEARS ENDED DECEMBER 31, 1994AND 1993

	1994	1993
CASH FLOWS FROM OPERATING ACTIVITIES		
net income	$ 42,185	$ 42,312
adj to reconcile net income to net cash prov by operating activities		
Depreciation and amortization	100,069	82,197
Deferred tax provision	(412)	2,412
Gain on disposal of property and equipment		(420)
Changes in assets and liabilities that provided (used) cash		
Trade and other receivables	(66,323)	(112,910)
Prepaid expenses	(123)	(99)
Deposits	6,650	(6,650)
Federal income tax	14,716	(2,500)
Inventories	8,192	(48,975)
Accounts payable and bank overdraft	(38,263)	(59,482)
Accrued expenses	(244)	4,148
Total adjustments	24,262	(142,279)
Net cash provided by (used in) operating activities	66,447	(99,967)
CASH FLOWS FROM INVESTING ACTIVITIES		
Payments received on notes receivable from stockholder	35,001	71,265
Additions to notes receivable from stockholder	(14,811)	(40,468)
Purchase of property and equipment	(74,329)	(14,017)
Patent costs	(3,954)	
Proceeds from disposal of property and equipment		420
Net cash provided by (used in) investing activities	(58,093)	17,200
CASH FLOWS FROM FINANCING ACTIVITIES		
Principal repayments of long-term debt	(8,354)	(92,233)
Borrowings on note payable		175,000
Net cash provided by (used in) financing activities	(8,354)	82,767
NET CASH IN CASH	0	0
CASH AT BEGINNING OF YEAR	75	75
CASH AT END OF YEAR	$ 75	$ 75

SUPPLEMENTAL DISCLOSURES OF CASH
FLOW INFORMATION
Cash paid during the year for:

Interest	$ 53,884	$51,868
Federal income tax	$ 0	$ 10,000

When we revisit the questions raised at the beginning of this section, we are focused once more on *what our real business is.* In the last sections, Maria Jacobs makes it quite clear that their emphasis on sales and distribution is beginning to pay off. They are fully staffed, and have generated many creative marketing concepts to increase their market penetration (which is already at 80% in the athletic division). Special Products' *real business* needs to change, as it is already doing, to address new markets with their products, or they will "bottom out" -- be the provider of choice in a limited market. The issue of strategic direction simply will not go away, and Special Products is coupling their R&D skills with expertise in sales and marketing to meet it head on.

According to Dr. Porter, "The strength of the company seems to be in Marketing and Production. The Sales and Marketing segment of the plan is a comprehensive description of both direct and indirect advertising methods. The trade shows, customer demonstrations, calendars, and author collaborations all would be expected to build sales. The more impressive aspect is that these activities also maintain a high level of direct contact with end users and others who can supply valuable feedback for product development.

Comments on Production encompass the quality emphasis, as in the two years of testing on headgear prototypes. Their rotation of employees promotes flexibility, as well as ownership of quality concerns. They also look beyond the short term by budgeting each year for replacement tooling. By utilizing "Just in Time" approaches for both raw materials and finished goods they are attempting to be efficient while meeting increasing customer demands for more production variations and customization."

Epilogue

Without detracting from the value and importance of the hard work, commitment, and creativity exhibited by the management team at Special Products, Inc., we nonetheless have to give the nod to just plain good fortune, enhanced by preparedness to leap on opportunities. Over the last two years, good fortune has played its role in Special Products' health, particularly in what appears to be a sea-change in terms of product liability. Frivolous claims have decreased and several pending suits, to which Special Products was named as an ancillary respondent, have been settled with no fault to the company.

Based on their product development expertise, the company has moved forward to create several new, widely marketable products and has designed more effective and efficient production methods. The net result has been a surprising increase in personnel rather than the feared reduction in force as a cost-cutting measure.

In fact, Maria Jacobs and the management team have renewed their commitment to development of personnel (which was not clear from the business plan). They had always believed in "bringing people along" on the staff and promoting from within. The result was a series of success stories: three employees (one from Colombia, one from India, and one from Rumania) who didn't know English when they began with the company ten years ago as production workers, are now supervisors and managers. Stories like these, that have become part of the company myth, generate a sense of belonging and security that enhances the effectiveness of their employees (and also makes the inevitable failures that much more painful to acknowledge).

As of today, Special Products, Inc. is in its third childhood, having redesigned itself, some of its products, and its focus on a new emerging market.

The real lesson to be derived from Special Products, Inc.'s experience is that we need not fear the unknown -- when we confront new possibilities and take the necessary risks that this implies, we create the opportunity for vastly enhanced profitability and for personal and corporate reinvention, a most satisfying epilogue to the ongoing small business adventure.

Chapter 6

———————————————▶

High Tech: From Clipper Ships to Computer Chips

Our desire for speed and efficiency drives us to create new technologies and to enhance the old ones. The clipper ship, so-named because of its ability to move along at a good "clip" and to "clip" time from long voyages, was popularized in the mid 1840's, and became a prized method of transporting gold from California and Australia during the gold rush period. The clipper ship was so fast that it was able to cross the Atlantic in less than 14 days and make the journey from New York to California, around Cape Horn, in 89 days (1854), a record that remained unbroken by a sailing vessel for 135 years, until 1989. Quite a technological feat.

The same desire for speed led to the development of electronic technology and rocketry, while the allure of efficient and flawless operations focused on feats of modern engineering and aviation. Competition in these fields is no less fierce than was the rivalry between the shipbuilders of Boston and New York City to create the fastest and largest clipper ships in the world, to better serve the burgeoning mercantile community. Elaborate claims were made by the masters in the shipbuilding field, and extravagant press releases survive to show us how very easy it is to get carried away by our own brilliant ideas. An entry in *The Maritime History Virtual Archives* advises us that the Stag-Hound, built in the late clipper era in Boston, was "a vessel designed with special reference to her builder's beau ideal of perfection in every sea quality." Not bad.

We can find a similar description in a modern print ad for Epson: "...the perfect combination of portability, brightness and versatility, you can now deliver dazzling presentations anytime, anywhere." Another proud claim by a purveyor of high technology.

But clipper ships ran afoul of the times. Less than 50 years separated their initial development as rum runners and their replacement by sturdier sailing ships (five-masters built to carry heavy cargo) and the invention of the steamship. Further, the opening of the Suez and Panama Canals, shortened the trips so that they obviated the need for speed over long distances.

And that signals the biggest challenges faced by high tech firms:

- How do we make a profit while our product is "hot"?
- Where do we get the money to build our prototypes?
- How can we protect our product from competitive copycats while awaiting patent?
- How do we stay one step ahead of the market and the competition?
- Can we scan the environment well enough to foresee imminent threats?
- And how many times can we do it?

The business plans that follow are for two companies -- one is based on computer technology and the other is an avionics engineering firm. Different markets, different products, different life cycle stages, varying levels of sophistication, vastly different sizes. One operates in an emerging market, the other in a mature market. Let's examine the way they've faced their challenges.

Case Example #4 - Quick Scan Inventory Systems, Inc.

Quick Scan Inventory Systems, Inc. is a very young firm, roiling in the turmoil of start-up issues. They have big plans, an idea for a product that they believe in, and a market that they perceive as large enough, growing quickly enough, and in serious need of their labeling system. Just six months prior to the writing of this plan, they had one employee, a net worth of less than $50,000 and 1993 pre-tax earnings of less than $50,000. Gerald Finkel was scrambling for customers, for development dollars, and for credibility, while doing the high tech equivalent of taking in washing on the side. His business plan is almost a fantasy, a description of where he wants to be rather than where he is.

QSIS' business plan shows all the hallmarks of a company in start-up. It is informal, has a simple structure centered around the owner, and it has a general feeling of anything goes. When a company is in start-up mode, it will focus on the very basics of business. You will want to include a **clear description of what you intend to do.** This can be harder than it sounds, especially if you're providing a service. You may begin with a discrete idea (like providing lawn care) that seems easy to define, with clear parameters. However, as anyone who has ever put together a business plan can tell you, the boundaries you set will likely be either too restrictive or too broad.

If they are too restrictive, you may find your business limited to cutting lawns, something you did in high school to raise money for the prom. If they are too broad, you may despair of ever fulfilling the mission you have set for yourself, overwhelmed by the variety of services you need to offer and the resources required for them. The ability to balance optimism with realism will help you to articulate your vision clearly and concisely.

Besides clarity of purpose, you will also want to aim for clarity of financial positioning. This means that your break-even forecast has to be practical, your cash flow has to be able to justify loan repayment schedules, and your accounts receivables have to be under control. If your enthusiastic optimism infects the plan at this stage, you can easily delude yourself into early failure. Because the sustainability of a start-up company depends on its flexibility, its responsiveness to a changing environment, and in great measure, its ability to obtain access to funding, overstatement of your own potential and anticipated financial returns of the operation can be disastrous. Thus, the role of the business plan for a start-up company is to provide guidelines for action, justification for existence, and a rationale to attract equity or debt dollars.

Gerald Finkel is inventing his company as he goes along, and using his plan as a series of stretch goals and benchmarks in the process of development.

Quick Scan Inventory Systems, Inc.

Business Plan

August 1, 1994

Prepared by
Gerald Finkel
President

Chapel Hill, NC

TABLE OF CONTENTS

EXECUTIVE SUMMARY

HISTORY

Quick Scan Inventory Systems, Inc. was founded in April 1993 to specialize in Warehouse Management Systems. The company's role in warehouse automation is to sell and install automated label applicators which print and apply bar coded labels to pallet loads of product. The bar code can be automatically scanned, which "captures" each pallet load and tracks each load throughout the distribution process.

The company supplements its sales and income by distributing thermal transfer (bar code) printers, scanners, verifiers, pressure sensitive labels, parts, ribbons, and software to industrial users. It also sells service contracts and performs service on a variety of label applicators, and thermal transfer printers.

The company identified the unique requirements of pallet load labeling and found no existing equipment performed satisfactorily and, therefore, designed application methods and equipment that performs very well. It has developed a prototype pallet load label printer/applicator and intends to produce and market this equipment.

MANAGEMENT SUMMARY

Gerald Finkel, President, has thirty-four years experience in sales, sales management, product development, and production management

Dave Morley, Technical Director, has six years experience in the packaging industry, specifically with label application equipment and printing systems.

Peter Vernon, Technical Service Manager, has five years experience in the packaging industry working with label application equipment and printing systems.

THE PRODUCTS

QSIS is a distributor of Thermal Transfer (bar code) printers, pressure sensitive labels ribbons, bar code scanners and software.

QSIS began production of its own labeling equipment in June 1994. The equipment's application techniques are new and specifically designed for pallet load labeling. Some of the components may be patentable and a patent search is presently underway.

THE MARKET

QSIS' market is a very narrowly defined niche referred to as Warehouse Management Systems (WMS). Its customers are generally Fortune 500 companies.

EXPECTED GROWTH

QSIS' goal is to produce and sell 10 units in 1994 and 300 units in 1999, which is doubling sales every year for the next five years. Our rationale for this projection is that no other equipment is available, at least at this time, that will consistently label pallet loads.

MILESTONES

Past
*   First quarter 1994 sales equaled 1993 total sales
*   Designed, fabricated and assembled prototype pallet load label printer/applicator
*   Secured first order for our label printer/applicator

Projected
*   Begin the manufacture of our own label applicators
*   Secure patents
*   Secure UL Certification and ISO 9000 Certification (Internationally recognized standard for quality)
*   Market equipment internationally

FINANCING NEEDED

QSIS is seeking an open line of credit for $125,000 for producing demonstration units, patent application, trade show preparation, and promotional material development.

LOAN SUMMARY

To date, the company has funded its research and development through retained earnings, while meetings its credit obligations on time.

QSIS is seeking an open line of credit of $125,000 for the production of two demonstration units, patent application, trade show preparation, and promotional media development.

Requested terms:
Term -- One year, renewable annually
Interest -- Market rate

Repayment -- Interest only on a monthly basis, with principal reductions as working capital permits Collateral will consist of the assets of the company.

This line of credit, together with a cash investment of $30,000 and continuing reinvestment of retained earnings will ensure that the company has adequate working capital to successfully launch its manufacturing operation. It will also assist the company in maintaining necessary cash reserves.

BUSINESS INFORMATION

Name of Company:	Quick Scan Inventory Systems, Inc.	
Building Location	Office	Manufacturing/ Assembly
	13567 Gouverneur's St. Chapel Hill, NC	Lake Industrial Park Chapel Hill, NC
Square Footage	1,000	2,500
Number of floors	One	One
Construction	Frame	Frame
Age of Building	26 years	26 years
Lot Size	9.3 acres	9.3 acres
Owned/Leased	Owned	Owned
Value	$145,000	$30,000
Payment	$775/month	-0-

QSIS provides its customers with a means of identifying their products so the products can be automatically traced throughout the distribution process. QSIS accomplishes this through the use of bar coded labels and the means to automatically print and apply the labels to its customers' products.

QSIS began operations as a distributor in April 1993.
QSIS' legal form of organization is an S-Corporation.
QSIS is owned by Gerald Finkel.

Quick Scan Inventory Systems presents a comprehensive overview of its organizational elements in the Executive Summary. Typically, a start-up will provide this sort of complete disclosure at the beginning of its plan, as part of its goal to create a sense of "existence" in its early ephemeral state. Based on the Executive Summary, we are expecting to read about a company that has a bright future and will be a good investment opportunity for us. How can we determine if this is really the case? The questions that we will want ask about the firm behind the plan will focus on cost of production, likelihood of establishing a sales beachhead, the ability to advertise and distribute the product effectively, and, most importantly, how risky is our potential investment.

Susan Fox-Wolfgramm, who teaches business policy and strategic management in the Business School at San Francisco State University, provides some questions for us:

- We are told that the company has secured its first order of its label printer/applicator but we do not know if sales have been made or how many companies have ordered the product. Currently, it is searching for a patent. How long will this take? Is it feasible?

- Management tells us that no other existing equipment in the market performs as well as QSIS's equipment. How do we know this? Performance data needs to be provided.

- Customers are generally Fortune 500 companies. Does the company have customers for its prototype or are these customers for the products QSIS is already distributing? Sure, orders have been placed but has any company actually used QSIS's label printer/applicator?

- Management has forty-five years (total) of experience in sales management, product development, production management, printing systems, label application equipment, and packaging industry; however, we need to know if these people have ever worked together as a team before or what their reputation is like in this industry. The technicians have much less experience than the owner. What is the organization lacking?

- Management's goals include: beginning the manufacturing of its own label applicators, doubling the sales of its own automated label applicators every year for the next five years, securing patents, securing UL Certification and ISO Certification, and marketing its equipment internationally. These goals need to be quantifiable, so that resource needs and time considerations are understandable.

- In order to meet these goals, QSIS is seeking an open line of credit of $125,000 for "producing two demonstration units, patent application, trade show preparation, and promotional material development. At this point, we do not know : (1) how much demonstration units cost to produce, (2) how long it takes to get a patent or if QSIS will receive a patent, (3) How easy or difficult it will be to become certified, and (4) what QSIS intends to spend on promotional activities and how far-reaching they will be.

- What has the company been doing for the year and four months it has been in business? Mainly research and development? Did it have any help in doing this? Does it currently sell competitors' label printers/applicators?   How much does a label/printer applicator cost to make? How large is the first order secured? How long will it take to secure a patent? What is the current demand for the product like?   Which countries does this company plan to market its product in?

MARKET ANALYSIS

Up to 1993, sales of non-printing pressure sensitive labeling equipment are estimated to be $25,000 annually, with print/apply labeling equipment estimated to be $47,000 annually, for a total of $72,000 annually.   These figures are based on research conducted by manufacturers of this equipment, and represent sales in the United States. It is noteworthy that printer applicators were not available before 1985 and sales were relatively insignificant until 1989. In the four to five year period 1989 through 1993, a $47,000 market emerged. This is due to the need for variable and bar coded information on labels.

Labeler Manufacturers and Distribution

Company	$ Volume	Method of Distribution
Avery/Dennison	22,000,000	Direct
Label Aire	12,000,000	Distributor
Willett Labeljet	12,000,000	Direct & Distributor
L.S.I.	6,000,000	Distributor
Lord label Co.	6,000,000	Direct
All Others	14,000,000	Various
Total Market	$72,000,000	

The Warehouse Management Systems (WMS) market targeted by QSIS is a new market. Our conservative estimate of its potential in five years is another $47,000,000. This estimate, at $24,000 per labeling system, accounts for less than 2,000 systems. When one considers the number of production lines and warehousing facilities, this number is indeed conservative.

Our estimate of labeling systems sales growth (due to WMS alone) over the next two years is $4,500,000. Assuming $1,500,000 will occur in 1994 and $3,000,000 in 1995, then the total market for label applicators in 1994 will be $73,500,000 and the total in 1995 will be $76,500,000.

QSIS' goal for sales of its labeling systems in its first year of manufacturing/assembling is ten (10) systems with a retail value of $240,000 or 0.3% of the total market. As market demand grows, QSIS' goal for its second year is 20 systems with a retail value of $480,000 or 0.63% of the total market.

By 1999 the market is estimated to be at least $120,000,000. QSIS is forecasting sales of 300 systems in 1999 with a retail value of $7,200,000. This will be 6.0% of the total market.

CHARACTERISTICS OF THE WMS MARKET

Type of Organization	Manufacturing -- Mainly food products
Size of Organization	Typically Fortune 500 companies
Location	Continental US and offshore
Type of Products	Typically food and beverage
Type of Buying	Decentralized and Centralized, depending on project and customer
Source Loyalty	Typically very strong due to desire to standardize on equipment purchases
Kinds of Commitments	Contracts and agreements

COMPETITION

Competitor Name and Location	% Share of Market	Estimated $ Sales	Sales Loss due to QSIS
Avery/Dennison Ohio	30.6	22,000,000	-0-
Label Aire California	16.7	12,000,000	-0-
Willett Labeljet Texas	16.7	12,000,000	-0-
L.S.I. New Jersey	8.3	6,00,000	-0-
Lord Label Co. Texas	8.3	6,000,000	-0-
All Others	19.4	14,000,000	-0-
Total Market	100.0	$72,000,000	-0-

The five major competitors differ mainly in their method of sales -- direct or distributor. Avery/Dennison and Lord Label have a direct sales force that also sells their label products. Label Aire and L.S.I. sell through distributors that are mainly label manufacturers. Willet Labeljet began its sales through a distributor network and then decided to augment those sales on a direct basis with negative results.

QSIS ADVANTAGE OVER COMPETITION

The competition's market is primarily equipment to label individual units -- bottles, boxes, cans and the like. All its equipment and application techniques are designed for specific products and product surfaces (flat, round, concave, convex, etc.). QSIS has developed a conforming tamp which will apply labels to irregular surfaces like bagged product (e.g. dog food), off center cartons on pallets, cylindrical containers, etc.

The competition's equipment requires that the item to be labeled be presented precisely to the label applicator. This is difficult (at best) with a 4,000 lb. pallet load QSIS has developed several application devices that effectively apply labels to skewed and irregular surface pallet loads.

Most pallet load labeling applications require that at least two adjacent sides of the load be labeled in order to scan the bar code in multiple storage positions. Competition must use two label applicators to accomplish labeling two adjacent sides. QSIS methods of application require only one label applicator to label two adjacent sides of a pallet load.

Competition's equipment uses custom controls. Changing customer and market needs require software development for competitions equipment to meet those needs. QSIS equipment is PLC (programmable   logic controller) controlled which reduces software development time significantly.

MARKET TRENDS

Product	Pressure Sensitive Label Applicators
Source of Data	Manufacturers of Label Applicators
Sales 5 Years Ago	$25 million
Current Sales as of December 1993	$72 million
Sales in 5 years	$120 million

SHARE OF THE MARKET

	Total Market $ Sales	QSIS Total $ Sales	Percentage of Total Market Sales
1st year	$76,500,000	480,000	0.63
2nd year	81,500,000	960,000	1.18
3rd year	90,000,000	1,920,000	2.13
4th year	102,000,000	3,840,000	3.76
5th year	120,000,000	7,680,000	6.40

MARKETING MIX STRATEGY

Product/Service
1.   QSIS equipment will be produced to ISO 9000 quality standards.
2.   QSIS service is excellent. The company is committed to continuously improve its level of service.

3. Inventory, as a percentage of sales, will be maintained at 10% of total annual retail sales in order to provide excellent customer service.
4. QSIS customer service plan is based on a high level of communication with its customers and a commitment to keeping its promised level of quality products and delivery schedules.
5. QSIS label applicators and methods of application are specifically designed for pallet load labeling.

Promotion

1. Advertising will be accomplished through word of mouth, direct to prospective customer contact, direct mail, specialty advertising and trade journal space advertising.
2. Sales to date are due to the selling efforts of the company's President, Technical Director, and Technical Service Manager. The company plans to establish a nationwide network of authorized distributors to sell and service its label applicators.
3. Publish relations and publicity type activities will be accomplished through new product releases in industry trade journals.

Distribution

1. The company's label applicators will be sold direct to users and through authorized distributors. Other products and services the company offers will continue to be sold on a direct to the user basis.
2. The company's present site location is adequate for its first year of manufacturing operation. When annual unit sales of its label applicators exceeds twenty, it will require expanded facilities.
3. The company has approximately 1,000 square feet for office space and 2,500 square feet for manufacturing and assembly.
4. The company's vendor list includes sixty-two suppliers from whom the company has purchased parts and fabrication of parts for its label applicator and labels, ribbons, printers, software and bar code scanning equipment for resale.

Pricing

Pricing of the company's products allows for different gross margins depending on the product or service. Historically, this breaks down as follows:

Product/Service	Gross Margin
Thermal Transfer Printers	40%
Labels and Ribbons	30%
Service	62.5%
Label Applicators	68.8%

The company's overall gross margin in 1993 was 40.6%.

The company offers credit terms to its customers. On those products it resells, terms are 2% 10 days, net 20 days. Industry average Aged Accounts Receivable is 48 days. QSIS average for 1993 was 29.2 days. On those products it manufactures (label applicators), typical terms are 50% down, balance net 20 days following installation of the equipment.

OPERATIONS

MANUFACTURING

The company manufactures label appreciating equipment. Most of the components are purchased from or fabricated by outside sources to the company's specifications. The company's role in the finished product manufacturing process is assembly and small scale fabrication. The inventory control system is part of the accounting software, Peachtree Complete Accounting for DOS. When parts or assemblies are received, the packing list is checked for accuracy. The job number is written on the packing list document that is then entered into the computer system. As the parts or assemblies are drawn from inventory, they are invoiced and automatically removed from the physical inventory.

Quality is maintained through selection of vendors who will follow the company's specifications either in manufactured parts or fabricated components. Quality inspection is performed on all parts received. After all components are assembled, cycle testing is performed on premises to assure that when the equipment is installed it will unction to the customer's satisfaction.

The operation is oriented toward production of standard units with custom options.

RETAIL

The companies' retail operation includes reselling thermal transfer (bar code printers, labels, ribbons, bar code scanners and related equipment to industrial customers. Most of the products can be drop shipped directly to its customers and the operation takes place at the company's office. Sales in 1993 were $91,595 with a gross margin of 40.6%. Sales for the first six months of 1994 were $176,360 with a gross margin of 41.9%. Estimated total sales for 1994 are $405,000 with a gross margin of 37.3%.

SERVICE

The company's service operation functions to support the equipment it sells to its customers. Sales in 1993 were $7,821. Sales for the first six months of 1994 were $7,044. The company expects its service function to grow at the same rate as its labeling equipment.

SUPPLIERS

Principal Suppliers	Location	Product	$ Volume YTD as of 6/30/94
"A"	Addison, IL	labels	24,722.08
"B"	Ellington, CT	ribbon	21,219.13
"C"	Carlsbad, CA	printers	17,311.27
"D"	Sunnyvale, CA	printers	7,2323.59
"E"	Dallas, TX	labels	6,140.43
"F"	Kalamazoo, MI	fabrication	4,030.00
"G"	Kalamazoo, MI	parts	1,987.77
"H"	Ft. Worth, TX	parts	1,693.64
"I"	Addison, IL	parts	860.89
"J"	Grand Rapids, MI	parts	600.00
"K"	Kalamazoo, MI	parts	564.70
"L"	Battle Creek, MI	parts	516.58
"M"	Kalamazoo, MI	raw materials	239.29

At this point in the business plan, I am beginning to get a little worried. Mr. Finkel seems to be doing a great many things, having both diversified and vertically integrated his operation. One of the traps that start-ups frequently fall into is the temptation to be all things to all possible customers. After all, we know how to do it, we have the technology, and nothing seems to be stopping us. We have a vision and we intend to make it real.

One danger sign that flashes from this plan appears in the "Characteristics of the WMS Market." Source loyalty is stated as "typically very strong due to desire to standardize on equipment purchases." What does this mean for the incubating company? We're told that the top provider of WMS items controls 30% of the market, the next two providers control an additional 33%, and the two beyond that control nearly 17%. This leaves a little over 19% for everyone else, and brand/source loyalty is very high. I wonder how to break into this market.

Reading a little further, I learn how much better Quick Scan Inventory Systems' product is than the rest of the providers. In fact, it is a completely different product, one that does not seem to fit in with the existing warehouse management model. Who has asked for this new development? Does anyone want it? I really need a more comprehensive market study before I'm willing to commit to this invention. When we discover that the equipment will be produced to ISO 9000 standards, yet the company needs $125,000 to produce its prototypes, the question arises of where the money to obtain ISO 9000 certification is going to come from. Big dollars are needed here, much more than the $125,000 that is being sought.

Here is where runaway optimism can run you straight into trouble. Dr. Fox-Wolfgramm enumerates some of the potential problems that Finkel may confront:

- Management assumes that this line of credit, a cash investment of $30,000, and continuing reinvestment of retained earnings will insure adequate working capital to "successfully launch its manufacturing operation and maintain necessary cash reserves." There does not seem to be any mention of an existing "cash cushion" for unplanned circumstances.
- Market research on the Warehouse Management Systems market, targeted by QSIS, shows that mainly food manufacturers compose this market in the U.S. and offshore. These are typically Fortune 500 companies who have strong brand loyalty, due to their need for customized equipment. Thus, they seem unlikely to hastily switch their warehouse automation systems to QSIS's system.
- QSIS claims that its advantage over the competition's equipment is that it requires only one label applicator versus two, and that it uses a

programmable logic controller, "reducing software development time significantly." However, we do not know such things as: (1) Would competitors even consider pursuing this technology (and they have more experience/resources)? (2) How much of an advantage does this technology offer companies over the industry standard? (3) What is the degree to which companies would be willing to switch to this new technology ? (market demand) and (4) How much would they would be willing to pay for it ?

- QSIS has a long vendor list, with vendors located pretty far away (e.g., Michigan, California, and Illinois, etc...). Right now, the company does not have any exclusive arrangements with suppliers, which would improve its inventory control efficiency. Pricing of products and service allow for different gross margins. How were these determined?"

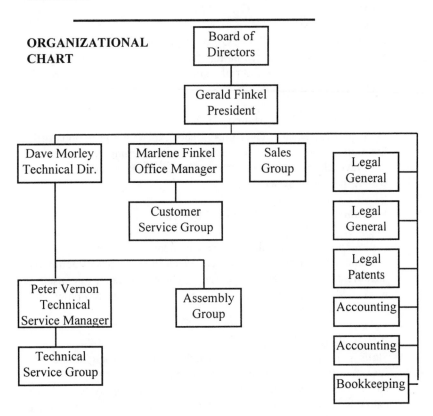

ORGANIZATIONAL CHART

Board of Directors

Gerald Finkel
President

Dave Morley
Technical Dir.

Marlene Finkel
Office Manager

Sales
Group

Legal
General

Customer
Service Group

Legal
General

Legal
Patents

Peter Vernon
Technical
Service Manager

Assembly
Group

Accounting

Technical
Service Group

Accounting

Bookkeeping

JOB DESCRIPTIONS

Position: **President**
Reports to: Board of Directors
Duties and responsibilities: Overall management of the company. Performs both the Marketing and Sales functions. Responsible for meeting company sales and profitability goals.

Person filling position: Gerald Finkel
Skills and experience: Thirty-four years experience in sales, sales management, marketing, product development and production management. During his career he has developed thirteen new products in pressure sensitive materials and pressure sensitive labels.

Position: **Office Manager**
Reports to: President
Duties and responsibilities: Manage all office procedures. Responsible for all accounting functions including Billing and Collections, Inventory Control, and Payroll. Also responsible for personnel record keeping.

Person filling position: Marlene Finkel
Skills and experience: Over thirty years experience in various office function positions. Has been instrumental in keeping detailed records that have allowed the company to find and correct initial problems with its computer system.

Position: **Technical Director**
Reports: President
Duties and responsibilities: Development of labeling systems., customer software, customer electronics, new equipment documentation and training programs. The performance of consulting work with the company's customers. The sale of equipment and service contracts.

Person filling position: Dave Morley
Skills and experience: Six years experience in the packaging industry, specifically with label application equipment and print systems. He has worked on various projects integrating labeling systems, PLCs, bat code scanners, sales, and product handling systems, from project inception through technical documentation, system installation, and

training. Experience with IBM-compatible PCs, as well as IBM, DEC, and HP midrange and mainframe systems. Developed packages and utilities using BASIC, Pascal, C, and dBASE IV. Experience with embedded systems and PLC programming. Strong in electrical, electronic, and mechanical design. Most recently, performed most of the design work on the commune's label applicator, redesigned the company's swing arm and conforming tamp, oversaw the fabrication of all parts, and successfully installed this equipment at The Quaker Oats Company.

Position: **Technical Service Manager**
Reports to: Technical Director
Duties and responsibilities: Assist in the development of labeling systems, custom software, customer electronics, new equipment documentation and training programs. The sale of service contracts and the performance of service.

Person filling position: Peter Vernon
Skills and experience: Five years experience in the packaging industry working with label application equipment, weighing systems, printing systems, and other packaging machinery. He specialized in field service system installation and training in addition to working with system integration, PLCs and bar code scanners. Excellent communication skills and training abilities.

A Passion for Planning

STATEMENT OF ASSETS AND LIABILITIES –
INCOME TAX BASIS
AS OF DECEMBER 31, 1993

ASSETS

CURRENT ASSETS

Cash	$1,488.00	
Accounts Receivable	5,404.00	
Due from employees	1,523.00	
Inventory	8,675.00	
TOTAL CURRENT ASSETS		$ 17,090.00
FIXED ASSETS		
Equipment	$7,564.00	
Furniture	2,656.00	
Less: accumulated depreciation	(6,660.00)	
NET FIXED ASSETS		3,560.00
Organization costs - net		2,689.00
TOTAL ASSETS		23,339.00

STATEMENT OF ASSETS AND LIABILITIES –
INCOME TAX BASIS
AS OF DECEMBER 31, 1993

LIABILITIES
& EQUITY

CURRENT LIABILITIES:		
Accounts payable	$ 6,401.00	
Payroll taxes payable	1,602.00	
Accrued auto allowance	4,160.00	
Accrued rent	6,400.00	
Note payable - Officer	21,198.00	
Note payable - RAM	978.00	
TOTAL CURRENT LIABILITIES		$ 40,739.00
STOCKHOLDERS' EQUITY		
Common stock		1,000.00
Current net income (loss)		(18,400.00)
Retained earnings - end		(18,400.00)
TOTAL STOCKHOLDERS EQUITY		(17,400.00)
TOTAL LIABILITIES/EQUITY		23,339.00

STATEMENT OF REVENUES AND EXPENSES –
INCOME TAX BASIS
FOR THE SIX MONTHS ENDING DECEMBER 31, 1993

	Year to Date	%
REVENUES		
Machinery	$50,670.00	50.96
Parts & Accessories	48,756.00	49.04
NET SALES	99,426.00	100.00
COST OF SALES:		
Machinery	11,624.00	11.69
Parts & accessories	47,438.00	47.71
TOTAL COST OF SALES	59,062.00	59.40
GROSS PROFIT	40,364.00	40.60
OPERATING EXPENSES:		
Salaries	12,311.00	12.38
Payroll taxes	1,139.00	1.15
Advertising	675.00	0.68
Auto expense	6,321.00	6.36
Dues & Subscriptions	349.00	0.35
Employee benefits	993.00	1.00
Entertainment	664.00	0.67
Insurance	3,482.00	3.50
Interest expense	590.00	0.59
Depreciation	6,660.00	6.70
Amortization	414.00	0.42
Miscellaneous expense	282.00	0.28
Office expense	2,189.00	0.28
Shop supplies	261.00	0.26
Postage	776.00	0.78
Professional fees	1,763.00	1.77
Repairs & maintenance	162.00	0.16
Telephone	5,298.00	5.33
Travel	8,041.00	8.09
Rents	6,400.00	6.44
TOTAL OP. EXPENSES	58,770.00	59.11
NET OP. INCOME	(18,406.00)	(18.51)
Other income & expense		
Interest income	6.00	0.01
NET INCOME (LOSS)	(18,400.00)	(18.51)

PROJECTED FINANCIAL STATEMENTS
FOR YEARS ENDING
DECEMBER 31, 1994
DECEMBER 31, 1995
DECEMBER 31, 1996

QUICK SCAN INVENTORY SYSTEMS, INC.
SUMMARY OF SIGNIFICANT PROJECTION ASSUMPTIONS
AND ACCOUNTING POLICIES

NATURE OF PROJECTIONS

These financial projections are based on two different sales levels and present, to the best of management's knowledge and belief, the Company's expected results of operations and significant changes in financial position for the projection periods of such sales levels are attained. Accordingly, these projections reflect its judgment as of August 14, 1994, the date of these projections, of the expected conditions and its expected course of action if such sales levels are attained. The presentations are for the purpose of obtaining potential bank financing for an existing corporation that is engaged in the manufacture of label applicators and the sale of parts and accessories (i.e., labels, ribbons, thermal transfer printers, software, bar code scanners and verifiers) related to these industry and service. Accordingly, these projections are not useful for any other purposes. The assumptions disclosed herein are those that management believes are significant to the projections. Furthermore, even if the sales levels are attained, there will usually be differences between project and actual results, because events and circumstances frequently do not occur as expected, and those differences may be material.

REVENUE

Management's goal is to produce and sell 10 label applicator units in 1994 and 300 units in 1999, which is doubling sales every year for the next five years. The company's label applicator has a retail price of $24,000. Projected sales of applicators in 1994 of $240,000 is estimated to represent only .3% of the total market for this type of product. The company supplements its sale and income by distributing thermal transfer (bar code) printers, scanners, verifiers, pressure sensitive labels, parts, ribbons, and software to industrial users. It will also sell service contracts and perform service on a variety of label applicators, and thermal transfer printers. A 50% deposit is required with purchase orders for label applicators and is reflected as a liability "customer deposits." It is assumed that it will take approximately 60 - 90 days to manufacture after receipt of an order and another 30 days to receive the balance of the sales price. Sales are recognized when received in full.

Total sales for the next three years are projected to be as follows:

	Worst Case	Most Likely
1994	$ 367,488	$ 438,204
1995	810,639	1,227,318
1996	1,894,935	2,572,556

Sales to date have been accomplished by the sales efforts of the Company's President, Technical Director and Technical Service Manager. The Company plans to establish a nationwide network of authorized distributors to sell and service its label applicators.

COST OF GOODS SOLD

The cost of label applicators is approximated to be 57% under the Worse Case Scenario and 52% under the Most Likely Scenario. Parts and Accessory costs are approximated to be 69% and 62% of sales, respectively. These percentages exceed what the company has experienced during 1993, which was approximately 31.2% for applicators and 40.6%, overall. Management has elected to use the slightly more conservative cost percentages in its projections.

OPERATING EXPENSES

Salaries:
Salaries are based on the following number of employees:

	Worst Case	Most Likely
1994	4	6
1995	6	8
1996	8	14

Payroll taxes:
Management has calculated payroll taxes at 7.65% of salaries.

Employee benefits

Employee benefit costs consist primarily of health, life and workers compensation premiums which vary with the size of the work force.

Insurance
Insurance costs are management's best estimate of general liability, hazard and product liability coverage.

OPERATING EXPENSES

Interest expense
Management is seeking a $125,000 line of credit for working capital. Maximum borrowings under the line are projected to be $100,000. Interest is being calculated at the rate of 15%.

Under Management's' "Most Likely Scenario" it is projecting an additional borrowing of $100,000 to finance the purchase of new facilities for $200,000 in 1996. Interest is also computed at 15%.

Depreciation
Expectation for the building depreciation is calculated using the Modified Accelerated Cost Recovery System which is an accelerated method used for federal income tax purposes. Under generally accepted accounting principles, fixed assets would be depreciated under the straight line method over their estimated useful lives. Equipment has a five year life, furniture - seven years, and the building - 39 years.

Amortization
Organization costs are being written off over a 60 month period. Patent costs anticipated to be incurred in 1994 are being amortized over 15 years.

Professional fees
Management has included in this category accounting and legal fees to be incurred as ordinary and necessary expenses for the ongoing

conduct of it business. No extraordinary fees for legal defense, patent costs, etc. are included in these amounts.

Rents
The company currently occupies a 1000 square foot office facility and a 2500 square foot manufacturing/assembly facility which it leases from its sole stockholder. Monthly rental is $8-- which included utilities, property taxes and insurance. The projections assume that his rent will be accrued but unpaid during the period covered by the projections. The rent will cease in July 1996 under Management's' "Most Likely Scenario" when it occupies its newly acquired facility.

CORPORATE ORGANIZATION

Management has selected to be an S corporation, whereby shareholders report their proportionate share of corporate income, losses, and tax credits in their individual income tax returns. The corporation will, therefore, incur no income taxes. The corporation will be subject to the North Carolina Single Business Tax. Management has not included an allowance for this tax in it projected operating expenses.

OPERATIONS

The company will depend mostly on outside sources for components to manufacture its label applying equipment. The company will use an automated inventory control system. Quality will be maintained through vendor selection, quality inspection of parts, and cycle testing of products. Again, this is essential to maintaining a good reputation in the industry. The operation is geared toward the production of standard units with custom options. Retail operations include reselling printers, labels, ribbons, bar code scanners, and related equipment to industrial customers. Sales have increased substantially since 1993 but gross margins have dropped about 2%. Why? This needs to be addressed. Service operations have dropped a bit in one year and are insignificant, compared to retail sales, but QSIS expects this function to grow at the same rate as its labeling equipment. Why?

The organization chart shows technical responsibilities (currently filled), sales responsibilities, professional services, and administrative responsibilities (currently filled), being held under a board of directors and the president. Once again, questions remain as to:

(1) How will sales be handled and by whom?
(2) Who will handle the professional services?
(3) Who are the members of the board of directors?

FINANCIAL

A CPA has prepared the historical financial statements for income tax and cash flow. These statements are as of December 31, 1993. Projection statements are included for the year endings of 1994, 1995, and 1996. Since this is an S Corporation, no provision or liability for federal income taxes is included in the financial statements.

In 1993, many red flags appear including: negative working capital, negative net income, negative stockholders equity, making it an extremely financially unattractive company which might have a hard time repaying a loan. Furthermore, no trends can be established yet, in terms of presenting more than one balance sheet or income statement.

Projected financial statements for years 1994, 1995, and 1996 show most likely and least likely scenarios with sales increasing but with corresponding increasing expenditures in salaries, benefits, insurance, etc... making it hard to convince potential investors that this is a good deal.

SUMMARY

QSIS has a premature strategic business plan for its future funding and growth. Consideration has been given to the basic details surrounding its brief past, present, and future which is good; however, there has not been much time to prove anything, let alone to develop a history of success. The product innovation is for a proposed high growth niche market but not one company has actually "used" it yet. Furthermore, the weaknesses of the business and its potential problems have not been addressed (e.g., no manufacturing sales yet, negative financial standing, lack of board of directors, etc...) and there are many questions left unanswered, with no letters of recommendation from industry analysts, etc., making this business a highly risky venture for a financial commitment at this stage. If QSIS addresses the points highlighted above, it should be able to make a more convincing argument for the financial resources that it needs.

Epilogue

Life can be funny. As is correctly pointed out in the commentary, there are abundant problems facing Quick Scan Inventory Systems, Inc. The most obvious of these is Finkel's belief that his new, unpatented and untried product will gain nearly instantaneous acceptance in a Fortune 500 market. No one will be surprised to learn that it didn't happen quite this way.

Although this business plan relates a story of a technological advance in labeling equipment, the truth is that that equipment never really made it very far off the drawing board. This is a classic case of an "overnight success" that takes years to come to fruition. After two years of going to a dry well, Finkel and his staff landed a major account "overnight."

The large, well-known company that became their first big account was more interested in QSIS' printer than their labeling equipment. QSIS had no intention of missing this opportunity for success, regardless of what the product may have been, so they built a prototype printer for their new client. The client ordered twenty of them immediately, with orders for sixty more to come.

Two long, lean years after the writing of this plan, QSIS' bank balance is moving upward and, without a single look backwards, Finkel is on his way to the big time in a totally unexpected direction.

After all is said and done, Gerald Finkel had the last laugh on the experts because he remembered the key rule for start-ups: You need to control your business plan —do not let your business plan control your business.

Chapter 7

———————————————▶

Three Versions of Growth

In the Chapter 4, we saw a manufacturing firm in the growth phase (Special Products, Inc.) begin to focus on streamlining organizational structure and selection of a strategic direction. Next, we will examine three versions of the growth phase in a high tech firm. In the following case, the first business plan for Aerotech Engineering Industries, Inc. focuses on issues of marketing, the second is a sales prospectus designed to attract outside investors, and the third is an additional effort at fund-raising in the wake of the previous plan's failure.

Case Example #5 - Aerotech Engineering Industries, Inc.

Aerotech Engineering Industries, Inc. (AEI manufactures and sells high tech products to a mature industry). It presents quite a different picture from the start-up firm we just examined. This is the story of an entrepreneur who wouldn't give up. For some 25 years, Jack Roselle refused to surrender to difficult bosses, corporate takeovers, foreign investors, and bits and pieces of the company being sold off or absorbed by others.

In 1967, when just a young engineer, Roselle went to work for AEI and developed an air data instrumentation process. About ten years thereafter, the owners began to sell off various sections of the business, having shrunk down to about $4.5 million in sales (from the $6-7 million they were selling before the defense industry cutbacks in the late 1960's). Roselle put together a financing package to buy the company, but the owners refused to sell to him for a variety of complex reasons. As Roselle tells it, "the two owners who had built up the business were like a bad marriage - they were not willing to sell for fear that one of them may benefit more from the sale than the other."

By the late 1980's, sales had grown from a low of $700,000 to about $5 million. Roselle tried to buy the company again, since the original owners now appeared ready to sell . They *did* sell, but not to Roselle. They sold to a British holding company, and it took another five years until Roselle was finally able to complete the purchase of his specialty area of AEI's operation. Less than five years have elapsed since Roselle took over AEI, and in that period sales increased despite the challenges of a continually shrinking defense budget. Roselle expects to take AEI to $20 million in sales by the year 2000 by constant reevaluation of priorities, a commitment to continuous improvement, willingness to change, and sheer personal strength. Although the United States has a $250 billion defense budget, less than $50 billion is for acquisition of capital materials. The continual merger and acquisitions of big companies has changed their perspective as well so that, although the customer base is increasing, overall industry sales are decreasing due to the number of competitive products being produced.

Each generation of technology brings with it the requirement to embrace change and, according to Roselle, "unlike fine wine or rare books, the defense industry does not improve with age."

AEROTECH ENGINEERING INDUSTRIES, INC.

BUSINESS PLAN #1 IN THIS SERIES

November 9, 1984
Revised January 23, 1985
CURRENT BUSINE8S STATUS

INTRODUCTION

Aerotech Engineering Industries, Inc. was organized in 1954 as a successor to a partnership formed in 1950 by its two principal officers, and became a public corporation in 1961. The company's initial and principal product in all the years through mid-1976 was a unique ultraprecision potentiometer, a primary position-sensing electronic component which had wide application in electronic analogue computers aircraft instrumentation, automatic process and Control systems, missile and space programs, communication and test equipment; in the late 1960's the Company began to manufacture its own line of aircraft and medical instruments using potentiometers and the then-emerging semiconductor-based electronic technology.

The aggressive use of low-cost offshore production by AEI's competitors which seriously eroded potentiometer prices in the early 1970's and the anticipated shift from analogue to digital modes of electronic instrumentation by many customers induced the Company to sell its major potentiometer product line in mid 1976. Subsequent to this divestiture the Company continued producing the high-technology aircraft and medical instruments portion of its former operations, which at that time had total annual sales of under one million dollars. Since that time the annual sales of these two product lines have grown to nearly four million dollars.

Aerotech Engineering Industries, Inc. continues to be publically owned with 72% of the common stock held by the two founding principal officers. In addition to its primary manufacturing operations, the Company also owns and operates industrial property adjacent to its main plant, formerly occupied by itself but now rented to others on short-term leases.

The Company functions in two operating divisions, each headed by a Vice-President; the Instrumentation and Controls Division (I&C), which manufactures and sells products of its own design based on advanced gas and liquid pressure sensing technology, and the Medical Division (Medical) which sells products of its own design and manufacture and private-label products manufactured by others for the measurement of cardiovascular functioning in humans and animals. Overall company management and the operation of company-owned real estate is shared by its two principal officers assisted, in accordance with the requirements of a publicly-owned company, by independent accountants and auditors, legal counsel, and stock transfer company.

DIVISIONAL SALES ANALYSIS
Instrumentation & Control Division

The I&C Division sells its products in two broad markets - the aviation field, both military and commercial, and the industrial marketplace.

Aviation Products

As described in the attached catalogs, AEI products for the aviation field consist of Air Data Instrumentation and Systems for aircraft

including Altitude and Airspeed Transducers, Altitude and Airspeed
Rate Transducers, Air Data Computers., Mach Number and True
Airspeed Computers, and Engine Pressure Transducers.   These
instruments are typically used in both manned and pilotless military
and commercial aircraft as part of the on-board stabilization, flight
guidance navigation and engine controls systems. These products are
fully qualified flight instruments usually manufactured to customer
specifications through direct contact between AEI engineers and the
customer.   Customers for AEI aviation products include the major
airframe and avionics companies such as Northrop Aviation Beech
Aircraft Lear-Siegler Corp., Sperry Corp, Jet Electronics Corp., etc.;
the potential number of customers totals some 40, including
government agencies.

The current U.S. markets for the aviation products manufactured by
AEI and for two other related products are shown in Table I; these
have been compiled from reports published by the leading aviation
and instrument publications (not shown here).

Medical Division

Since its formation, the Medical Division has been involved in the
Cardiovascular Diagnosis field, initially with the development and
supply of an advanced electrocardiograph machine and a line of
cardiac data acquisition consoles for computer-assisted ECG analysis
to both the U.S.Public Health Service and several leading proprietary
medical instrument manufacturers on a private label basis. A variety
of cardiac data acquisition and telephone transmission products were
subsequently developed and manufactured in connection particularly
with after-surgery pacemaker patient care. In addition to equipment
sales the Company entered the business of distributing private-label
recording charts to the medical profession and hospitals, typically for
use on AEI medical recording devices.

Medical Division emphasis in recent years has been in the direction of
meeting the need for self-diagnosis and monitoring of cardiovascular
function by cardiac rehabilitation patients and others, particularly in
the exercise and fitness areas where public awareness and interest has
grown enormously The basic instrument sold by AEI for this purpose
is a heart rate monitor, or pulsemeter, used typically by an individual
while exercising on a stationary bicycle, rowing machine treadmill,
etc. or while walking or jogging, as a medically approved means for
guiding the intensity of exercise to safely achieve maximum health

benefit.

No validated statistics are available for the size of the current market for pulsemeters. The potential customer base can be determined from the following reported by Frost and Sullivan, a leading market survey concern:

Running shoe sales were 19 million pairs in 1983 compared with 9 million pairs in 1977. Stationary exercise bicycle sales were 2.4 million units in 1983 as compared to 600,900 in 1977. Rowers, treadmills, and weight machine sales in 1983 totaled 2 million units versus 100 000 in 1977. 12,000 commercial health and racquet clubs operated in 1983 as compared with about 1,500 in 1977.

The Medical Division now sells from stock ten different types of heart rate monitors or pulsemeters to a present nationwide network of over 600 dealers in the exercise equipment fitness and health fields; it also sells component parts and complete instruments to several exercise equipment manufacturers for incorporation into their own products. Pulsemeter sales are currently at the annual rate of 15,000 units compared with 500 units in 1977. The Company competes with seven other suppliers.

All instruments sold by the Medical Division were originally of its own design and manufacture. To meet the rapidly growing demand for pulsemeters, late in 1982 the Medical Division began to sell pulsemeters manufactured on a private-label basis by others for AEI. In 1983, some 40% of the total Medical Division Instruments sales were in private-label items; in 1984 these amount to 75%.

Reading this section of the Aerotech business plan may leave you stunned. It is dense, complex, and difficult to follow. The biggest stumbling block for high tech firms when developing a business plan or other narrative document is style. Although the information that is provided is comprehensive and instructive, after reading it we may still be unsure of the content. Essentially, the plan reads as if it were written by engineers. This is natural, because it *was* written by engineers. Engineers are trained to provide technical and specific information in a logical sequence, and to do so in a manner that does not distract other engineers. In much the same way as lawyers are trained to communicate with other lawyers using contract language that makes for dull reading for the rest of us, technical experts don't waste time on frills or seek out metaphors to enhance their prose. This is unfortunate, because investors and other interested outside parties are more likely to be attracted to a readable document than to one that is difficult to follow. Let's see what happens when we move to the marketing plan section.

MARKETING PLAN

Instrumentation & Control Division

Existing Aviation Product Markets

Aerotech Engineering Industries is an established business, well-known to the industry as a supplier of high quality, high performance instrumentation and controls. The Company is listed as either a sole source or approved source in many customer drawings and specifications and as such is a part of the regular cycle of procurement by customers, receiving both solicited and unsolicited requests for proposals and bids for the supply of existing products and new products. This factor of strong goodwill established over many years of successful supply coupled with aggressive marketing enables AEI to confidently plan for and reasonably expect future profitable growth.

The market for I&C products is broad and non-seasonal. In general the I&C Division manufactures its products under fixed price contracts with deliveries to start 30 to 150 days after purchase order receipt and completed within a few months thereafter. Payment terms are usually net 30 days.

As a consequence, a close correlation exists between order backlog at the start of any calendar year and the actual sales (shipments of product) generated in that year.

Existing Industrial Product Markets

The marketing plan for I&C industrial products is aimed at establishing customer recognition for AEI products in those niches where AEI can secure dominance. The AEI low pressure sensors and bubbler systems are just such products. The AEI low pressure, high precision sensor fits in particularly well in the ventilating and air conditioning field and the bubbler systems are particularly suited for the handling of difficult fluids. Technical advertising, trade show and new products releases to trade publications have been focused on these areas. New sales literature has been prepared, existing sales representatives have been particularly trained to service customers with such applications and new sales representatives have been added to broaden the customer base for these products. The sales growth of I&C industrial products is expected to continue with sales in 1986 expected to be 30% ahead of 1985, and the same trend of growth into 1987.

New Aviation Product Markets

The sales of aviation products currently in production total a small fraction of the market which in itself is growing, and consequently the company does anticipate its sales of these products to grow as greater market penetrations are made. However, a somewhat larger market exists for that related product lines, Central Air Data Computers and Pitot/Static Tues. Entering these new markets is the purpose of the company's current market plan for I&C Aviation products

The company is uniquely positioned to enter these markets because these two product lines are horizontally related to the products currently being manufactured. Pitot/Static Tubes located on the exterior of the aircraft connect directly to AEI Air Data Sensors and these sensors typically are connected directly to the Central Air Data Computer. Thus, entering these tow markets is a form of horizontal diversification in which the company already has a credible technological foundation and customer recognition.

To guide the company's entrance into these markets, the company has engaged a particularly well-qualified engineering and marketing consultant. This consultant has had many years of experience both as a designer and user of these kinds of aviation products and has a wide range of personal contacts in the engineering and procurement departments of the major aircraft manufacturers and related government agencies.

New Industrial Product Markets

The company's sales of I&C industrial products constitute a very small fraction of the market and consequently the company does anticipate its sales of these products to grow as a greater market penetration is made. To reach new customers in new markets the company has embarked on a program of horizontal product line expansion in which those products currently being produced are being reconfigured to meet the requirement of previously untapped markets. For example, a basic low pressure sensor supplied to the environment control industry has been restructured in a stainless steel configuration for mounting through cooking vessel walls to meet the stringent sanitary requirements of the food processing industry. Initial customer acceptance has been favorable and sales in 1986 are expected to total $100,000 for these items. Also in 1985, the I&C Division developed a unique instrument for the measurement of liquid density based on its established Bubble Systems. The measurement and control of liquid density is essential in many chemical and drug processes. The AEI Density Bubble System enabled the company to enter this market with a unique relatively low cost instrument. The annual market for density measurement instruments is estimated to be $8 million. Sales of this AEI device in 1985 were $75,000, growing to $299,000 in 1986.

MEDICAL DIVISION
Existing Markets

Estimates are that twenty-five to thirty million people in the United States are now including some form of regular exercise as part of their lifestyle and that some four million units of exercise machines such as stationary bicycles and rowers, treadmills, etc., are sold annually, numbers that are projected to continue to grow at a rate of 20 to 30 percent annually. Since the Company's primary medical product line, heart and pulse rate monitors are typically used by the exercising public as an accessory to an item of exercise equipment, the Medical Division's market effort has been principally directed through telemarketing to retailers of exercise equipment from whom the consumer purchases equipment. These include general sporting goods outlets, specialty exercise equipment shops, home health care retailers and bicycle dealers. Catalog mail-order specialty houses are also solicited and an ancillary marketing effort is directed to the manufacturers of exercise equipment to whom private label or customized OEM pulsemeters are supplied. While the individual end-user ultimately becomes the purchaser of these products, the Medical Division does not solicit retail sales except where no dealer is available to the consumer.

The total number of retail outlets for sporting and exercise-related merchandise is reported by trade journals to be:

General Sporting Goods Stores	45,000
Specialty Exercise Equipment Dealers	10,000
Home Health Care Outlets	5,500
Bicycle Dealers	6,500

A large number of these specialize in sporting apparel, game implements, or other software; others handle only token amounts of exercise machines or the kind of equipment such as dumbbells or weight machines for muscle building which does not involve pulse monitoring. The net number of dealers currently likely to handle Medical Division products are:

Medical Product Markets

General Sporting Goods Stores	4,000
Specialty Exercise Equipment Dealers	2,000
Home Health Care Outlets	1,500
Bicycle Dealers	300

New Markets

The strong dealer network so far established for Medical Division products offers a large initial sales base for any new products which are introduced. For example, the Medical Division is currently investigating the sales potential of other health aids and diagnostic devices only obliquely related to exercise which can be distributed through its dealers, while certainly such products are attractive to the existing dealer's customers, by their uniqueness in a sporting goods or exercise equipment environment may introduce a new type of customer to the dealer and so enlarge his market.

There is also a recognition that while exercise and fitness has been pictured as a young people's game, there is a large and growing older persons segment of the public which has special needs with regard to exercise and fitness. These needs include specially designed exercise machines, cardiac rehabilitation devices and instruments, and other health aids. For example, exercise machines that produce cardiovascular benefits (aerobic) for bedridden or limited mobility individuals are currently being designed to accommodate these special needs. To a limited extent the Medical Division has made entry into this market with Pulsemeters through its Home Health Care dealers. This initial entry has revealed an extremely large sales potential which is somewhat geared to the third party reimbursement (Medicare) limitations. To insure success in this market requires the endorsement or other participation of the health care professional. Seminars on exercise and fitness for professionals in the cardiac rehabilitation and geriatric care field are planned for 1986 to promote the prescription of Pulsemeters and special exercise machines.   Endorsements from recognized authorities will be sought.   The impact of this program on Medical Division sales will be limited in 1986 but is expected to contribute significantly to sales in 1987 and beyond.

Finally, in 1985 the company devised a totally new concept in portable heart-rate monitoring devices which represents a technical breakthrough in both performance and ease of use, with unique market appeal to all types of users; applications for U.S. and foreign patents have been filed.   Development models are in current design and pre-production prototypes will be available early in 1987.   Full scale marketing is projected to begin the last quarter of 1987.   Sales of this new product in excess of $1,500,000 are projected for 1988.

Financial Plan

Since its major restructuring in 1976, the company has largely financed its growth out of earning and has no significant long term debt.   The company has a $500,000 open line of bank credit at prime interest rate which it utilizes in the form of short term loans to finance swings in inventory, payables and receivables;   no loans are outstanding at this writing.

Companies that produce non-consumer products are unlikely to describe them in flashy or sexy terms. The assumption is that rational decision-making will make sales -- a better product, one that is more efficient, more reliable, or more accurate will sell itself. This assumption is false. Purchasers rarely have all the information they need to make a "good" decision. Purchasing decisions are made in an environment of limited knowledge and imperfect competition, a condition referred to by economists as "bounded rationality." The wise marketer will, therefore, present products in a manner consistent with the corporate philosophy or mission, and not be afraid to show emotion, enthusiasm, or commitment.

In the case of AEI, corporate philosophy revolves around quality, so their marketing efforts must be aimed at potential customers who purchase quality rather than price or speed. When sales are dependent on responses to Requests for Proposal or bid documents, the marketing process may shift to an emphasis on price, after minimally acceptable levels of quality are met. Engineering quality depends on consistency in design and production. This may create complications when developing different sorts of products for very different markets, as AEI does. Maintaining a consistent marketing strategy thus presents significant challenges.

John Trinkaus, engineer and business planning specialist, suggests: "While both segments of the marketing plan contain the essential detail which one would reasonably expect to find, it is offered in the form of hard, basic cold facts, devoid of any fleshing out and arrayed in a sequence that is perhaps more suggestive of an engineering document than a management piece. While there is nothing inherently wrong, nor dysfunctional, with such an approach, attention only to the hard, rather than to both the hard and soft, issues is to needlessly forego some measure of potential worth of the resulting plan through incompleteness.

For example, it is often useful to relate specific plans, such as a marketing plan, to the strategic plans of the firm. Will the attainment of what is envisioned in the marketing plan be instrumental in achieving an established objective of the firm -- for instance, increased profits, increased market share, or enhanced economies of scale? It is important that the reader not perceive any loss of unity of direction and coordination of function. Then too, it is generally helpful to both reader and writer to unfold a progression of logic rather than a simple offering up of facts--the pieces have to be fitted together to form a composite.

Detailing the "how" is also a useful technique -- exactly how things are to be done. Such detailing not only helps to ascertain do-ability as the plan is being prepared, but can later serve as a source of benchmarks to gauge how effectively the plan is being carried out. Implementation is an important function that should normally be included in a marketing plan for, all other things being equal, it is generally more important than the vision of what is to be done. It need not be treated in exact detail, but should be sufficient to generate confidence in the reader that the writer recognizes its significance and appears to have given thought to how it might best be done. In some measure the AEI plan does do this, but perhaps not enough.

There are a number of things missing, in whole or in part, the inclusion or completion of which might well have strengthened AEI's plan. For example, how much will the effort cost, how is it to be funded, and what is the supporting rationale? What is the time frame involved? Here some type of diagramming might be useful. It could be a simple Gantt chart, which would not only help with the planning itself but provide assistance as well with the control function when the plan is being implemented. Also, is there any contingency plan, or fall back course of action -- what triggers it and what are the implications of putting it into place?

On balance, the plan appears acceptable for its intended purpose -- the entry into new markets and the introduction of new products. However, the mix is off. The piece does appear to be overly engineering-oriented and light on the management aspects. This is not necessarily bad, but at times it can make the difference between a suitable work and a good work. In view of such factors as a highly competitive marketplace and a rapidly changing environment, it would seem to make sense for a business to try to acquire as much competitive advantage as it can, in everything that it does, especially when there is little or no cost to achieve such a benefit."

The second AEI business plan is a sales document, that is, the goal of this plan is to raise money for the purchase of the business by two vice presidents, Edward Mansfield and Jack Roselle. Written a year and a half after Plan #1, this plan "looks" more like a traditional business plan than the first plan in this group.

BUSINESS PLAN #2
Aerotech Engineering Industries, Inc.
June 1986

Aerotech Engineering Industries, inc. (AEI) is a 36 year old company with established products, customers, and no outstanding debt. Company philosophy has been guided by its original two owners, who control 70% of the outstanding shares. These two owners are ultra-conservative managers who are independently wealthy. In 1967, AEI sales were in excess of $8,000,000 and selling on the American Exchange for over $40/share. In 1976, they sold the two primary product lines for $1,400,000, the proceeds of which were distributed as a liquidating dividend. The residual corporate shell with more than 50 employees had sales of $1,100,000 with the current product lines constituting about 70% of that total. Further divestiture of two additional product lines have left the company with its current two operating divisions, Medical products and Instrumentation and Control (I&C) products. These two divisions are managed and operated by AEI's two vice presidents, Edward Mansfield and Jack Roselle, who also share in corporate management responsibility.

The vice presidents have been told by the two principals that the company is for sale and that they are actively looking for a buyer. The principals have been treating the company as an annuity; yet in spite of their philosophy of making minimal investment in future growth, Mansfield and Roselle, with contracts tied to profits in three year cycles, have increased both sales and profits.

This is a business plan of how the two vice presidents of AEI, each of whom presently owns 5% of company stock, propose to purchase AEUI and to manage the company as a profitable high growth-oriented company.

(repetitive material deleted here)

The products of both the instrumentation and control division of the medical division are directly traceable from design concept through marketing and sales to the division vice presidents, Mansfield and Roselle, both of whom have bachelor's and master's degrees in engineering and one of which additionally holds an MBA.

With the sale by the two principals and their subsequent retirement there will be a 30% increase of corporate profits based on their 1985 remuneration. Part of this $300,000 cost saving will be used by the new management to hire the long-needed staff to ensure continuous AEI growth, Particularly a strong financial manager and additional sales and engineering to support the marketing program.

This business plan is based on a sale price of $4.50/share asked by the principals. Mansfield and Roselle anticipate that the actual tender will be between $3.50 and $4.50 per share. The plan requires an outside investment of $1,500,000 and a $5,500,000 loan with a six year term. The plan projects a continuous compounded corporate sales growth of 20% a year with gross profit margin paying back the $5,500,000 loan required for this purchase within six years. The investors who will be putting up the $1,500,000 dollars will, at the end of six years, have 40% equity in a 20 million dollar company showing a 20% profit margin.

The plan also anticipates the strong possibility that in 3 to 4 years a public offering could be made to provide for early retirement of the loan debt and high return on investment.

Aerotech Engineering's enormous potential has not been realized due to the founding principals' management and their repeated failure to invest in the future. The new management team of Messrs. Mansfield and Roselle, utilizing AEI's capabilities, reputation, and favorable acceptance of its products, will successfully lead the company through this large growth period to the benefit of all investors.

THE NEW COMPANY AFTER THE LBO

The two divisional vice presidents of Aerotech Engineering Industries are seeking to buy the corporation through the means of a leveraged buyout. Assuming the LBO comes to fruition, Mansfield and Roselle, the two current vice presidents and operating division managers, intend to work as a team to convert the corporation from one that is directed by ultra-conservative managers, who are treating the company as an annuity, into a creative dynamic corporation that aggressively markets its products and plans and invests for tomorrow. With its established products and loyal customer base and with the new dynamic management team of Roselle and Mansfield, AEI will grow from a five million dollar corporation in 1985 to a twenty million dollar corporation by 1992.

Both Mansfield and Roselle, who serve as corporate vice presidents and as division managers, have been able to increase AEI's sales and profits in spite of the two founding principals' philosophy of making minimal investments. Roselle and Mansfield are positive that with their management and organization, the company will show both high profit and high growth. Detailed plans of how the Medical Division will increase from a 1985 sales of $2.9 million to a 1992 sales of $7.9 million, and how the Instrumentation and Controls (I&C) Division will expand from $3 million in 1986 to $13 million in 1992 is described in this Plan.

The LBO assumes a sale price of $4.50/share as asked by the principals. This plan requires an outside investment of $1,500,000 and a $5,500,000 loan with a six year term. If the negotiated price is $4.00/share Roselle and Mansfield intend using the $0.50/share differential to purchase the current plant building occupied by AEI and now owned by the wives of the two current principals. Additionally an option to lease or buy an adjacent 20,000 sq. ft. building will be negotiated to provide space for planned expansion. The plan projects a continuous compounded corporate sales growth of 20% a year with gross profit margin paying back the $5,500,000 loan required for this purchase within six years at 12% projected interest. The investors who will be putting up the $1,500,000 dollars will, at the end of six years, have 40% equity in a 20 million dollar company showing a 20% profit margin.

Roselle and Mansfield also anticipate the strong possibility that in 3 to 4 years a public offering could be made to provide for early retirement of the loan debt and high return on investment.

This earnest and optimistic beginning is supposed to set the stage for a confident description of a company ripe for investment. According to Dr. Trinkaus, Mansfield and Roselle may be starting off the mark:

Concerning the executive summary, which is the first hurdle, AEI's plan is limited. While it does aim to keep the reader reading, and highlights some of the significant issues, overall it is not clear and to the point. Rather than using short and simple language, and choppy bullet-type phrases, it is relatively long winded and complex. Messages in the AEI plan almost have to be pried off the pages rather than having them fly off by themselves. Consequently, "opportunity", which should be the basic message, does not come through loud and clear. Money people generally have lots to do and not much time to do it. Consequently, it is prudent to capture their interest up front -- but if that can not be done, then avoiding turn-offs and pitfalls is certainly a necessity.

Using only a few pages, employing a crisp, clear, and concise writing style, it is important that the first thing the reader encounters is a captivating executive summary -- something that does not raise eyebrows or red flags. While the emphasis should be substance, style and form are certainly important. It has to *read* good, in addition to *sounding* good. While it can certainly be too slick, if there is to be an error in judgment as to the degree of polish, it is perhaps better to overshine than undershine. It is important to get the reader's attention quickly, stimulate interest, raise desire for involvement, and clearly spell out what action is being sought.

What is probably needed is simply a recognition of whom the plan is being written for. While it is certainly being prepared as a part of a necessary planning endeavor, helping the firm with such things as keeping it tuned to its environment and establishing long term objectives and short term goals, it has a more immediate use -- in this instance, the obtaining of capital. Hence, it should be formatted in keeping with the jargon and operating practices of the financial sector. While an engineering orientation is fine, unless things are clear for the money people, and the sought after capital obtained, it really does not matter how good the technical portions are as they will never come to pass without the front-end capital.

Who are the people involved in this venture? Why should we trust Mansfield and Roselle with our money? What's the corporate structure? Where are they going?

BIOGRAPHIES OF PROPOSED PRINCIPALS
(abbreviated versions)

Edward L. Mansfield

Edward Mansfield, currently employed as Vice President of Aerotech Engineering Industries, manages and operates the Medical Division. Mr. Mansfield joined AEI in 1966, as an electrical engineer with five years industrial experience mainly in the defense field. At AEI he has served as project manager, chief medical engineer, sales

A Passion for Planning

manager, division manager, and was appointed corporate Vice President in 1981.

Edward Mansfield received his Bachelor of Electrical Engineering in 1961 from Polytechnic Institute of Brooklyn, MEE in 1964 from New York University, and his MBA in 1970 from Bernard Baruch College of City University of New York.

Jack Roselle

Jack Roselle, currently employed as Vice President of Aerotech Engineering Industries, manages and directs the Instrumentation and Controls Division and participates in corporate management. Mr. Roselle has directed the engineering group that has developed and designed the state of the art airborne instrumentation and ultra low pressure sensors, giving AEI an edge over larger and stronger competitive companies.

Mr. Roselle was recruited to AEI, in 1967, as an electrical project engineer with seven years of experience in design and marketing in aerospace and industrial electronic instruments and systems. At AEI he has served as chief instrumentation engineer, division manager, and was appointed corporate Vice President in 1981.

Jack Roselle received his Bachelor of Electrical and Electronic Engineering in 1961 from Massachusetts Institute of Technology (MIT) and his MSEE from Polytechnic Institute of New York in 1967. He has further taken many post graduate courses in engineering management at C.W. Post. Mr. Roselle has served as President of the Seattle/ Tacoma Chapter of Instrumental Society of America and chairman of the IEEE Seattle Section of Cybernetics and Robotics, he is currently a member of the MIT Education Council.

NEW FINANCIAL MANAGER

To achieve dramatic increases in sales and profits it is essential for the management team to properly utilize all of its resources, especially those provided by a dynamic financial manager. It is the intention of Mansfield and Roselle to employ such an individual who will also function as corporate controller. This key member of our management team will relieve us of our current requirements of performing credit checks,, preparing and presenting cost audits, invoicing government customers, regularly arranging for salesmen commissions, negotiating with vendors, overseeing purchasing, supplying and supervising the transmittal of corporate financial data to customers, and the monitoring of the accounts receivable to insure that AEI is paid in a timely manner.

A strong financial manager who understands the corporate business and is able to generate timely and accurate financial operating information will make management easier for Roselle and Mansfield. The corporate financial staff will assist in preparing proposals, evaluating sales, and identifying potential problems. Mansfield and Roselle intend to employ a financial manager who will help the company grow rather than just record data. Such an individual will most likely be a recent MBA who previously had spent 5-10 years as a corporate controller before returning to school for his MBA.

MEDICAL INSTRUMENTS

EXISTING MARKETS (see Business Plan #1 for description of market)

MEDICAL PROJECTION

The Medical Division, which has grown from $1,100,000 in 1983 to $2,300,000 in 1985, projects sales of $2,800,000 in 1986. The primary products provide Heart Rate Monitors and Pulsemeters which measure a person's heart before, during and after exercise. During this entire growth period the Medical Division has been managed and directed by E. Mansfield. With the hiring of the strong financial manager and minor reorganization of staff responsibility, E. Mansfield, who has assumed many accounting responsibilities, will be able to increase his time devoted to sales and marketing from approximately 50% to 75% of a typical work week. His remaining 25% will still be shared between general corporation and management responsibilities.

The current philosophy of maintaining a limited number of high quality, high profit products will be retained. New products will be added to service additional requirements of heart rate monitoring applications. One new device will store heart rate data for 8 to 16 hours (one work shift) and interface with a computer for heart rate trend analysis for various industrial, institutional, municipal and corporate applications to measure capabilities under physical and mental stress. Applications for this new unit will include monitoring policemen and firemen while on duty, union members in hazardous occupations, high school and college athletes while on the playing field and medically concerned individuals. Furthermore, to reduce potential liabilities and to inexpensively identify poor athletic risks or predict when an athlete starts to become aerobically deconditioned, computer trend analysis of the workout versus heart rate is essential.

This heart rate trend monitoring application is achievable by modifying an existing product. Mansfield and Roselle have identified the application but it has not yet been addressed by AEI. Hardware and software to satisfy this heart rate trend monitoring requirement could be market ready in 1987. Similar equipment can also be used to sample an individual's heart rate during the course of a normal day for the purpose of determining heart rate irregularities. More sophisticated equipment such as halter monitors, which are leased at a cost of approximately $275 per day, are currently used for this application by the medical community. Even though the proposed AEI product is not as diagnostically complete as the halter monitor, the potentially high profit diagnostic fee and anticipated retail price of less than $400 will insure a market for this device starting in late 1987 or early 1988. Another heart rate monitor including data storage capability but without computer compatibility will be marketed to the ever increasing aerobic dance field at an anticipated retail price of $99 to $149 starting in 1987.

The aforementioned new family of products and markets together with the anticipated growth of the self-health monitoring field as the population ages and becomes even more electronically oriented will result in a medical division growth in excess of 20% compounded from 1986 through 1992.

This 20% growth can only be accomplished through an aggressive marketing program to which both Mansfield and Roselle are fully committed. The sales staff will be expanded to enable us to service our retail outlets regularly and maintain our strong customer loyalty. AEI's asset of having one of the largest, loyal and knowledgeable distribution networks in the sophisticated high quality exercise field will be capitalized. Allied products will be introduced through our telemarketing network. The pulsemeter and heart rate monitors will be targeted to Yuppie and Senior Citizen markets where the need for obtaining optimum cardiovascular benefits in the least amount of time has been clearly established and is currently being stressed throughout the media. Sales Representatives will also be added as required to service large retail outlets that do not operate successfully through telemarketing.

To administer this high expansion, new off-line computerized sales reports will be generated. Determining the profitability of an account and evaluating a salesman's performance will become standard procedure. Within one to two years a full order entry and invoice system will be installed to reduce paper work costs and further enhance customer service.

The growth of AEI's Medical Division was based on product recognition within the trade which was obtained by attending many trade shows and advertisements in trade magazines. It is Mr. Roselle's intention with Mr. Mansfield's concurrence that this trade policy will continue with the accent being on teaching the retail outlets product benefits and selling techniques. Simultaneously, it is new management's intention to obtain more consumer recognition of products through supplying retail outlets with more effective point of purchase displays and posters. Dealers will be made part of team and will be continuously educated and informed about current and new products. The product benefits to both dealers and their customers as well as various sales closing techniques will be disseminated to AEI dealers on a regular basis.

Consumer direct order advertising will be evaluated in 1987. New Management will expand direct mail order marketing if the test marketing results are positive. Additional consumer product recognition will be a side benefit of this mail order sell.

Research and development for the Medical Division will consist of a continuous search for new products, the review and evaluation of product functions and negotiation and trading ideas with vendors. Significant new business is anticipated starting late in 1987 and continuing through at least 1991 from a new patent pending heart rate monitor specifically designed for the jogger, conceived by E. Mansfield and under exclusive development by Sanyo Corporation for AEI. E. Mansfield and Roselle further intend to attend foreign shows for the first time in AEI's history with the intention of actively pursuing products prior to their entrance to the U.S. market.

To assure that the expansion and profitability goals are simultaneously met, the new management expects all salesmen in addition to bringing in profitable business to work as a team and report all competitive information particularly pertaining to pricing, delivery and new products. Salesmen through management directives, will teach the outlets how to best present products.

The present facilities have to be expanded in 1988 to accommodate the increase in staff associated with the projected growth. Additional space requirements will depend upon which future allied products are added and whether they are primarily small electronic instruments similar to current pulsemeters, or if the new products are more mechanical in nature like bicycles, rowers or treadmills.

INSTRUMENTATION AND CONTROLS

The instrumentation and controls (I&C) division designs, manufactures, and sells pressure related electronic instruments which observe, measure, or control, the parameters upon which modern industry and aircraft are vitally dependent.

The I&C division is subdivided into two broad market groups: airborne instruments and non-airborne instruments. In both market groups the products are sold to military and commercial customers. In 1985 with I&C sales of $2,840,431 the distribution of the market was 2/3 airborne, 1/3 non-airborne; military sales were 50% of the combined total. The markets for I&C products are growing in all areas (i.e. military airborne market growth is greater than business aviation shrinkage). Our sales at this time are less than 1% of the market in any area (references Frost & Sullivan, Aviation Week And ISA reports) and a minuscule percentage of the total market. The I&C division's instruments have an excellent acceptance among our present customers. The current management has discouraged investment in medium and long range sales/marketing programs. New management by changing marketing philosophy from order taking to aggressive selling, will force both near and long term corporate potentials to be realized. In addition, Mansfield and Roselle are better prepared to work harder, accept new challenges, follow opportunities, and invest in the future than are the current owners.

The plan for growth of the I&C division under new management, is to increase I&C sales of our current and new instruments to more than $13,000,000 in 1992. It is also our intention to continuously search for that big opportunity for a large development or manufacturing contract in our area of expertise. Over the next six years, a staff increase of 10 salesmen and 12 engineers is budgeted.

The increase in staff will change our ratio of engineers to salesmen from 4:1 to 2:1 in consonance with the new emphasis on aggressive marketing. This growth will be accompanied by the development of new instrumentation in our present business areas and in the development of a horizontal diversity of products.

I & C's principal goals:
1. Increase growth of pressure based products to sustain a 30% per year compounded growth from 1988 to 1992.
2. Maintain a 20% sales profit ratio.
3. Maintain an R&D program of about 5% of sales to provide new product growth.
4. Develop closer relationships with customers, especially in airborne products, with the objective of increasing both vertical and horizontal growth.

Airborne Instrumentation

The airborne instrumentation market is the one which new management has identified as providing the largest corporate potential for growth. The biggest factor in achieving this growth will be Roselle's and Mansfield's expenditure of corporate resources to market the product; therefore, we have budgeted our largest staffing increase to this product area. New management plans to increase both sales and engineering staffs by at least one or two people in each of the next six years, Airborne product market sales are normally achieved by a combination of close customer contact supported by technical proposals. The time element between initial identification of requirements and product delivery is normally two to four years, resulting in projected sales and growth of:

YEAR	SALES	GROWTH
1986	$2,200,000	
1987	$2,500,000	14%
1988	$3,100,000	24%
1989	$4,200,000	35%
1990	$5,400,000	29%
1991	$7,500,000	39%
1992	$10,400,000	38%

This growth plan has been developed based on maintaining our current products and developing new ones within the vertical market of air-data transducers. These products are components which sense air pressures around an aircraft and develop parameters proportional to aircraft flight such as altitude, and airspeed. AEI's largest customers use these products for flight control of RPV/DRONE/TARGET aircraft, for manned aircraft and for helicopters.

AEI has a good reputation for product performance and quality and has developed close relations with many of our larger customers. These customers have all told us that by spending more time at their facilities we will be in a position to receive a significant increase in business. Sales visits to these major corporations will be scheduled bimonthly instead of annually or every 18 months. Current AEI ownership has discouraged this type of missionary travel. New management will increase sales by direct sales call to our potential airborne customers. The typical sale for these products is between $25,000 and $400,060 dollars justifying this activity.

Almost all of the airborne instruments are customized to meet particular customer needs and wants. The specifications often require different attitudes, power excitation, and/or color. For this market AEI will continuously try to satisfy customer needs by adapting existing products or designing new ones. The costs of a typical product consist of 25% material and 10% direct labor of selling price. The support engineering costs are burdened as part of overhead, and additionally amortized over the first few orders for a particular product. Thus each product we supply does carry its burden of engineering. We do not anticipate that the nature of this market will change. It is the market which will provide AEI's greatest long term growth. The non-airborne products will be derived from the airborne instrumentation technological advances.

There are a number of new products currently just being completed or under development which will be increasing our product base. They, with closely related derivatives, will provide a good stepping stone for additional sales. One new product, an air-data computer model 8800M, less than 1/2 the size of our model 8800, has been sold in prototype quantities to three new customers. It is used in helicopter and target drone autopilots, and with aircraft engine trend monitoring systems. A derivative product using the internal assemblies as a stand alone system will be sold to the flight data recorder market as the next generation replacement of products AEI is currently manufacturing. Another new variation of our model 8800 is now being tested for one customer for use as a reporting altimeter. The circuitry developed for this application is 100% adaptable for a new series of AEI altimeters with altitude reporting capability. This type of new product development now directed by J. Roselle at a cost of about 5% of sales has been the basis of past AEI growth and will continue under new management. A major change will be that AEI will now budget about 8% of sales to actively market these airborne products.

The potential for product expansion in the airborne field is large and AEI, with dynamic new management, is in an excellent position to capitalize on both our technical expertise and on our customer base to develop lines of products in related horizontal markets. New management intends to investigate and pursue a number of products in these related horizontal markets for future growth. Examples of horizontal product potential are:

(highly technical section deleted)

Non-Airborne Products

The non-airborne product group manufactures products for the process control and energy control industries and low pressure sensors sold for military applications. Both of these large markets are quite competitive and salesmanship is paramount. New management intends to increase low pressure sensor sales by immediately hiring one salesman who will limit his selling efforts to models 5300, 5400, and related systems that new management has targeted for expansion. The target markets are the military which uses the 5300 in vehicle and shelter air filtration systems, and the energy control industry which uses the 5400 for variable air volume control, and furnace draft control.

(technical section deleted)

The non-airborne product diversity will be reduced to a set of standard products, resulting in an elimination of 20% of our current non-airborne sales. This will reduce the engineering drain caused particularly by low dollar ($500 -$3000) custom engineered industrial products, and permit completion of the two new models 5650 and 7700P/L. New management directions under Roselle and Mansfield will change the corporate emphasis to the promotion and marketing of the standard products in our product line.

New non-airborne industrial products will have the potential for being a product which can be built in some minimum quantity (25-50 unit lots) and whose expected sales volume will exceed $100,000 annually. This same criteria will be applied to existing products to determine their economic viability. The company will still retain its ability and willingness to respond quickly to new opportunities, and will continue to provide good customer support, but will not continue as a custom job shop selling valuable engineering resources without production potential.

Within I&C products, new management has identified the model 5700 and high pressure versions of model 5525 as items which will be dropped from our product line. Standard models of our bubbler system products 7600, 7700, 7800 will be defined so that these can be built as products not custom systems.

In keeping with the above guidelines J. Roselle expects to have a new product designated, model 770OP/L, under design in late 1986 with development completed by mid 1987. The 770OP/L is a portable battery operated instrument for measuring the density of liquids. This instrument incorporates novel technological ideas in its design and a patent application has been filed. To our knowledge the 770OP/L is unique in the market. A prototype has been built and is now under evaluation in Japan by a potential stocking distributor. Roselle is currently conducting a formal marketing survey of domestic catalog holders to evaluate industry interest in this instrument. The current density instrument market is $80,000,000 a year and if the prototype evaluation and market survey interest is positive, we will proceed with instrument production design.

Sales projections for the 7700P, based on initial product requests which prompted the building a prototype sample are:

1987	$403,000
1989	$280,000
1990	$420,000

Unit price is projected at $1400 for a field unit and $1800 for a more accurate laboratory unit with an output for continuously recording liquid density. There is a strong possibility that the 7700P will turn into a star product, but it is too preliminary at this stage to predict.

Mansfield and Roselle have budgeted 5% of non-airborne sales for advertising and product literature support. This will provide consistent exposure of our products to the targeted markets, and supply a large quantity of fresh leads to the commission sales representative organizations engaged to conduct direct customer sales.

(a section of growth projections and an optimistic financial projection is deleted here)

Mansfield and Roselle are in love with engineering. This is a fine thing for engineers, and a less positive attribute for managers. The job of management is to run the business, focusing somewhat less on professional interests and more on the tasks that the people who are going to fund their purchase are most interested in. That means making a strong case for quality of management, rate of return, and assets.

Some of the supporting material that Mansfield and Roselle need to make their case is missing. As Dr. Trinkaus, says, "To raise money, the plan must sell the concept to those who have the money. While conventional wisdom suggests that this is best done by talking about how good the product line is, the growth potential of the industry, and all the money it might be possible to make, those who have the money are normally more interested in other things. Bankers want to know about the firm's fixed assets and the collateral that can be offered to secure a loan. Venture capitalists, who are generally less conservative than bankers, are interested in the size of the return that can be made on their investment, how fast, and how big a piece of the business they can obtain for their money. Private investors normally want to know what's in it for them, and when are they going to get their money back. Consequently, what they all look to first are the financials -- the current and pro forma income statements, cash flow statements, and balance sheets.

The AEI financial statement coverage is thin, when contrasted with its treatment of the engineering details of the firm and its actual and proposed product lines. While this is understandable as the two officers are engineering folk, it does not mean that excellent technical coverage can substitute for good treatment of the financials. What probably should have been included, in addition to the current financials, are financial projections for the next 5 years: by months for the first two years, quarters the third year, and yearly for the last two years. Such pro formas need to be realistic and well thought out -- those in the business of buying pieces of businesses or lending businesses money, are not dumb, are not easily distracted from the pragmatic and do not buy on the basis of pie in the sky reasoning. Right after the executive summary, money people generally go straight to the financials. If the plan does not pass muster at this point, that's the end of it. There is no more. Even though the rest of the plan may be great, it's just not read."

By 1992, Jack Roselle had learned a lot. His next plan, identified as a Funding Proposal, covers much of the same ground as the two previous plans, but it handles the issues differently. Roselle is now stepping out on his own, Mansfield's interests having already been sold by FLP, PLC, the holding company that purchased AEI in 1987. He begins the plan with a clear statement of purpose and a concise description of his goals and potential payback. The plan has become more readable, more interesting, and more coherent. The company begins to sound more appealing to investors, especially once the financials are displayed. It appears that Roselle kept the interests of his potential readers in mind while writing this third plan.

Business Plan #3 of this series

Aerotech Engineering Industries, Inc.: A Funding Request
March 4, 1992

Executive Summary and Acquisition Objective

This business plan describes an investment opportunity that Jack Roselle, currently President of Aerotech Engineering Industries, has of buying AEI and expanding it into a larger more profitable Company. One of the necessary steps in this plan is to find an equity investor (or investors) who will invest $750,000 for a 33% share of the Company. This plan shows how this equity partner will achieve greater than a 35% annual return on his investment over five years.

Aerotech Engineering Industries designs and manufactures sensing instrumentation used in aircraft (75%) and in industrial process control (25%). Current sales are $3.8 million. The Company with a history of profitable operation sells mature proven products to established customers. AEI maintains an excellent reputation as a quality supplier to all its customers. The Company has recently enlarged its marketing staff and is successfully expanding its customer base by evolving and developing new products. This sales effort and added customers will be the basis of its future growth.

AEI was sold to FLP, plc, a British holding company in 1987 to facilitate the retirement of the two major principals. During the past 4 years Aerotech Engineering Industries has been one of the most profitable FLP companies. A marketing conflict with the major supplier of Pulsemeters for the Health and Fitness division of AEI resulted in the sale of that division to the supplier. This sale has left the remaining Aerotech Engineering Industries with products which are sold predominantly to the aircraft industry, a market not within the FLP strategic core business. FLP, therefore, wants to divest itself of AEI and has as a first step offered Jack Roselle an opportunity to purchase the Company. The estimated purchase price will be $2,100,900, consisting of 50% assets and 50% goodwill.

Following the management buy out of AEI from FLP plc, Jack Roselle maintains that by establishing the strategy of growth through increased sales efforts the full potential of Aerotech Engineering Industries can be developed. The objective is to be a profitable major manufacturer of quality specialty instrumentation. As this goal is achieved, AEI will be in a position to pay back its equity owners through an IPO, sale, or buy out.

Jack Roselle
President

INTRODUCTION

AEI's business has grown from $600,000 in 1977 to $2 M in 1987, the year of FLP's acquisition, to $3.8M in 1991. AEI's position in the market and its technical capabilities have enabled the Company to form a respectable business base from which, under new ownership, it will grow significantly during the next five years. This growth will continue through the decade.

AEI's instruments and systems serve two very different markets --the aerospace market for flight control instrumentation and the industrial process market for measurement and control of liquids and gases. Though both businesses are based on related technologies (sensing pressure), their marketing requirements are vastly different and the strategies adopted develop both businesses as separate entities. In the past, this has been a great advantage for surviving various business cycles. Both markets will continue to contribute to Aerotech Engineering Industries growth.

The two markets have been divided as follows: seventy-five percent airborne instrumentation and twenty-five percent non-airborne business. We believe that AEI is capable of expanding its industrial business, along with the continued growth of airborne products and customers. The strategy is to concentrate the industrial business on

A Passion for Planning

standard products while continuing to develop special function products for the aircraft market.

In presenting this plan it is worth recapping on our strategy: "...to focus on specific market opportunities and technological developments to ensure AEI becomes a broad based supplier of advanced technology components to the aerospace industry."

To achieve this goal, AEI has developed a product strategy to meet the needs of a diverse and large market. At the same time we are significantly increasing our customer base, away from a reliance on a few major customers.

In this plan, we will show how:
1) The successes of the past 24 months are moving AEI towards an extended period of growth.
2) The additional steps to be taken during the remainder 1992 and 1993, enabling us to reach our strategic goals.
3) A redefinition of our 'products' will ensure AEI focuses on its strengths in its niche product areas and markets.

The business plan has two sections covering separately the airborne and industrial non airborne business.

INVESTMENT ATTRACTIONS

_Established Profitable Business.** Aerotech Engineering Industries is a functioning profitable business with capable management, an experienced staff, and an established customer base and product line. Our sales staff currently has a greater number of outstanding quotations, proposals and new business prospects than at any other time. Our young engineering staff has recently completed a number of new designs for ongoing funded military programs and for the new industrial standard products. Engineering is now busy with new programs.

Product Designs and Sensor Technology AEI has many mature products which are designed to meet both industry and specific customer requirements. With an average product life of seven years current product designs represent about seventeen million dollars of future sales. The intellectual properties of the design include many proprietary production processes unique to sensor manufacturing.

Recognized Name. Aerotech Engineering Industries has been in the instrument business for over 40 years as a supplier of specialty instrumentation in various fields. Among its customers it has distinguished itself from its competitors through its flexibility of design and in its high level of customer service. In expanding our customer base this good reputation has enabled us to be accepted easily by new customers.

Quality and Reliability. AEI Quality Assurance System conforms to the requirements of MIL-Q-9858A, Weapons SPEC-6536, MIL-STD-2000, and MIL45208. AEI has all the necessary tools to meet the most stringent modern quality requirements. Our facility is certified by our customers who require that we comply with all the latest quality and reliability methods. Our staff is certified through special instruction and testing. Many of our products are fully qualified permitting other products to be certified by similarity.

Small Business. There are two potential benefits of the acquisition of Aerotech Engineering Industries by Jack Roselle. That it will be a small business and hence have a number of preferential sales advantages. A very large market area which would be open to AEI as a designer/manufacturer will be the replacement of older aircraft flight control instrumentation parts for the U.S. Air Force. This potentially would add ten percent additional growth rate to this plan. The second benefit is that as a U.S. owned Company, AEI would be able to obtain security clearance which would reopen part of the Airborne market not available to us as a FLP company.

FINANCIAL REVIEW HISTORY AND ACQUISITION PLAN INTRODUCTION

AEI is owned by FLP, plc a British holding company, through its US subsidiary. Since its acquisition by FLP in November 1987, CIC operated with two divisions, Instrumentation and Control, and Health and Fitness. The two divisions shared facility, accounting and administrative staffs. Instrumentation and Controls sells products of its own design and manufacture. Health and Fitness was an importer/distributor of pulsemeter heart rate monitors, an outgrowth of an earlier CIC designed product. In July 1990, CIC moved to a new 20,000 square foot leased facility in Seattle, WA. On January 2, 1992 the assets of the Health and Fitness Division were sold to Polar Electro OY, its major supplier. The H&F group moved to a new facility February 28th, 1992.

The ongoing Aerotech Engineering Industries, Inc. will be absorbing all of the previously shared facility, accounting and administrative costs. The staffing has been reduced to minimize the impact of these additional costs to the ongoing business and variable cost factors will continuously be reviewed. The financial figures presented herein reflect these increased costs on the ongoing operation of Aerotech Engineering Industries, Inc. Overhead and G&A ratios are shown to decrease with time reflecting the fixed costs associated with this downsizing of operations. The present facility is leased through September 1994. It can accommodate all the business growth planned through 1997. We are trying to sublet 5,000 to 7,500 square feet of excess space, which in today's realty market may take several months.

The financial projections for the acquisition include the following:

1. Statement of Income (P&L) for the continuing operations for the years 1988-1991.

2. Projected Income Statements for 1992 - 1997. The assumptions of cost and growth are on top of this chart.

3. Projected Cash Flow for the years 1992 through 1997 showing the cash flow, scheduled loan repayments, and a dividend payment to cover taxes assuming CIC becomes a sub-chapter S Corporation.

4. Below the cash flow chart is a Schedule of Bookings necessary for the sales projection planned.

5. Projected Balance sheets for the current year and through 1997. This shows the planned growth of retained earnings to $5,143,000 (before dividends) at the end of 1997.

Roselle is starting to make a good case. Aerotech Engineering Industries, Inc. sounds like a company with management that knows where it's going. Roselle has come into his own as President, and appears to be opening from a position of confidence. He knows how to describe AEI's strengths and he has selected a strategic focus, quality, as his defining philosophy. Even his writing style has tightened up and made a stronger impression. The introduction makes me want to read further, and look at the numbers.

FINANCIAL STATEMENTS

Projected income Statements for the Continuing Aerotech Engineering Industries, Inc.

The Company will be purchased through a combination of a bank loan of $600K secured by assets, a deferred payment of $750K from FLP, a $200K capital investment by Jack Roselle, and a $750K equity investment which this plan is requesting.

The assumptions for this plan are provided at the top of the page. The driving factor is maintaining a sales growth of 15% per year. The market for AEI's products is very large and we have demonstrated our ability to profitably compete. The sales force will achieve the bookings required and the management design and production organizations are in place to produce the products to achieve this sales growth.

The Projected Income Statement shows profitable growth planned for the Company during the next five years. Operations are planned to continue in the Seattle facility for that period of time. Overhead and G&A ratios improve as we fully utilize the facility and associated equipment and staff. The assumptions made for this plan provide for the expansion required to support this continuing growth. All projections assume an annual 4% inflation.

Statement of Income for the past four years

The income statement shows the historical performance of the business as has been reported and audited by Ernst and Young and by FLP, plc. It shows a continuing record of increased orders and a continuous increase of operating profit.

Sales in 1991 showed a slight decline due to a switch to "just-in-time" delivery by three of our major customers. This adjustment should not recur.

Cash Flow

The statement of cash flow for the ongoing operation shows a positive cash position and full repayment of borrowing. Dividend payments reflect the tax obligation to owners of a sub-chapter-S corporation.

Bookings/Backlog

The Company's products are built to order and the delivery schedules are typically between three months and a year and a half. The Company normally operates with a half year backlog. This table shows the required bookings and scheduled end of year backlogs needed.

Projected Balance Sheet

The projected balance sheet starts at the anticipated sale closing date of May 1, 1992 and continues through December 31, 1997. It shows the starting equity of $950K growing to a pre-tax equity of $6093K (before dividends) after five years with all borrowing repaid.

The Company will be in a positive cash position during this period while supporting a growing inventory and staff.

These projections are based on the operations continuing to run as they have historically. I plan that private ownership will improve all aspects of the company's operations, resulting in increased profits.

ASSUMPTIONS OF FOLLOWING PROJECTIONS:

SALES GROWTH PER YEAR	15%
LOAN BALANCE OUTSTANDING	$1,350,000
INTEREST RATE	9%
COST INCREASE PER YEAR	4%
MATERIAL COST AS % OF SALES	23%
DIRECT LABOR INCREASE PER	$180K
INCREMENTAL SALES	$20,000
ENGINEERING INCREASE PER YEAR	$42,000
SALESPEOPLE INCREASE PER YEAR	$40,000
ADMIN PERSONNEL INCREASE PER YEAR	$15,000

PROJECTED INCOME STATEMENT 1992 - 1997 ($000'S)

	1992 BUDGET	1993 FORECAST	1994 FORECAST	1995 FORECAST	1996 FORECAST	1997 FORECAST
SALES	4,180	4,807	5,528	6,357	7,311	8,407
COST OF SALES						
MATERIAL	961	1,106	1,271	1,462	1,681	1,934
LABOR	367	455	558	678	818	980
OVERHEAD	1,150	1,196	1,244	1,294	1,345	1,399
TOTAL	2,478	2,757	3,073	3,434	3,845	4,313
GROSS PROFIT	1,702	2,050	2,455	2,924	3,466	4,094
SELLING EXPENSES	658	724	793	865	940	1,017
ADMIN EXPENSES	511	546	583	622	661	703
ENGIN/ TECHNOLOGY	282	335	391	448	508	571
OPERATING PROFIT	251	444	688	989	1,357	1,803
INTEREST EXPENSE	61	114	90	66	41	17
PRETAX PROFIT	190	330	598	923	1,315	1,786

I & C DIVISION
STATEMENT OF INCOME FOR YEARS ENDED 1988 - 1991 AS REPORTED

	1988	1989	1990	1991	PROFORMA 1991
ORDERS	2554	3901	3337	3998	3998
SALES	3000	3129	3834	3756	3756
COST OF GOODS SOLD:					
MATERIAL	818	730	980	774	774
LABOR	281	295	306	300	330
OVERHEAD	941	915	1131	1083	1209
TOTAL COGS	2040	1940	2417	2157	2313
GROSS PROFIT	960	1189	1417	1599	1443
SELLING EXP	261	322	514	553	587
GEN & ADMIN EXP	380	319	352	372	544
R & D		132	132	132	132
OPERATING PROFIT	319	416	419	542	180

PROJECTED STATEMENT OF CASH FLOW 1992-1997 (000'S)

	1992 FORE CAST	1993 FORE CAST	1994 FORE CAST	1995 FORE CAST	1996 FORE CAST	1997 FORE CAST
CASH. BEG OF YEAR	200	304	196	197	359	768
PRETAX PROFITS	190	330	598	923	1315	1786
DEPREC/ AMORTIZ	87	73	73	73	73	73
(INC) IN A/R	(100)	(51)	(120)	(138)	(159)	(183)
(INC) IN INVENT,	36	(79)	(90)	(103)	(115)	(129)
PURCHASE OF FIXED ASSETS	(50)	(50)	(50)	(50)	(50)	(50)
INC. IN PAYABLES	87	55	70	50	75	75
DIVIDEND PAYMENT	(67)	(116)	(209)	(323)	(460)	(625)
CASH AVAILABLE FOR LOAN REPAY	384	466	467	629	1038	1715
PRINCIPAL REPAY	(80)	(270)	(270)	(270)	(270)	(270)
CASH, END OF YEAR	304	196	197	359	768	1525
CUMULATIVE REPAYMENTS	80	350	620	890	1160	1350
BOOKING/BACKLOG	1992 BUDGET	1993 FORE CAST	1994 FORE CAST	1995 FORE CAST	1996 FORE CAST	1997 FORE CAST
BACKLOG, BEG/YR	2100	2644	3040	3496	4021	4624
BOOKINGS	4724	5204	5984	6882	7914	9101

	PROJ 4/30/92	PROJ 12/31/92	PROJ 12/31/93	PROJ 12/31/94	PROJ 12/31/95	PROJ 12/31/96	PROJ 12/31/97
SALES		4180	4807	5528	6357	7311	8407
BACKLOG, END YR		2644	3040	3496	4021	4624	5318

PROJECTED BALANCE SHEET 1992-1996

	PROJ 4/30/92	PROJ 12/31/92	PROJ 12/31/93	PROJ 12/31/94	PROJ 12/31/95	PROJ 12/31/96	PROJ 12/31/97
CASH	200	304	196	197	359	768	1525
ACCT REC	650	750	801	921	1060	1218	1401
INVENT'Y	725	689	768	858	961	1076	1206
OTHER	30	30	30	30	30	30	30
TOTAL CURRENT ASSETS	1605	1773	1795	2007	2410	3093	4162
FIXED ASSETS-NET	272	250	250	250	250	250	250
GOODWILL	911	896	873	850	827	804	781
TOTAL ASSETS	2788	2919	2918	3107	3487	4147	5193
ACCOUNTS PAYABLE	300	350	400	450	500	550	600
ACCRUED	188	225	230	250	250	275	300

EXPEN NOTE PAYABLE TO BANK	600	520	400	280	160	40	0
NOTE PAYABLE TO THD	0	0	0	0	0	0	0
ROYALTY PAYABLE TO FLP	750	750	600	450	300	150	0
CAPITAL STOCK	950	950	950	950	950	950	950
RETAINED EARNINGS	0	190	520	1118	2041	3356	5143
ACCUM. 35% DIVIDENDS	0	(67)	(182)	(391)	(714)	(1175)	(1800)
TOTAL LIABIL. & EQUITY	2788	2919	2918	3107	3487	4147	5193

AEROTECH ENGINEERING INDUSTRIES, INC. SALES GROWTH

AIRBORNE MARKETS

AEI's markets address many different sectors of the aerospace industry. The current product range services the military's pilotless (drones) and piloted aircraft, the commercial aircraft market, and retrofit programs introduced as a consequence of changes in FAA regulations. Figure 1 projects the market segments AEI addresses currently and through the period of this plan.

A customer history profile is shown in Table 1. Each year through 1990 shows a dominant customer (1990 Northrop, 1989 Fairchild, 1988 Beech) accounting for 25% or more of the company's sales. The sales activity to expand the AEI customer base has been effective as shown in the 1990 & 1991 results. The Company expects to maintain the historical level of sales to most current customers and develop new customers of similar size. The company anticipates its main growth will come from the new generation of products with digital communication capabilities to an expanding customer base.

PRODUCT PROFILE (not included here)

TABLE I CUSTOMER PROFILE SALES (customer information not provided here)

TABLE 2 PRODUCT HISTORY (not included here)

COMPETITOR PROFILES (not included here)

TECHNOLOGY PROFILE

Aerotech Engineering Industries, Inc. is a company which designs application oriented sensor based instrumentation. Our designs use the latest state of the art analog components to achieve needed stability and accuracy. New AEI designs will incorporate microprocessors into new sensing instrumentation to meet new customer requirements. This change will evolve as fast as sales opportunities occur.

AEI sells its capability to design and adapt our instruments to meet specific customer requirements, cost effectively, within customer required schedules. For aircraft and military instruments, we provide the skills to build instruments to a high level of quality with documented controls and procedures. AEI has the skills to design the highly reliable instruments which will special skills in design of sensing instrumentation provide us with a growth core of instrumentation technology based on pressure measurement. This provides us with a niche in the air-data, pressure, level and flow instrument market. To support the products designed, we are highly skilled in electronic design (mainly analog - but are developing good digital electronic skills) , electronic packaging and test. We intend to use these skills in the growth of new sensor technology and in adding communication and control capabilities to our instrumentation.

I have eliminated a great deal of technical material in this version of the plan because it was reproduced earlier. However, the technical material remains in the original. It is easier to read here and easier to understand, but it is not of interest to the readers of the plan, who are financial people. The technical sections could appear as appendices, supporting the professionalism of the organization. This would allow Roselle more visibility to impress his potential funders with his managerial skill and ability to bring a good return for them. The financials could also benefit from some increased sophistication supporting Roselle's claims.

Dr. Trinkaus contends that to support what is fundamentally a sales prospectus, the three conventional financial statements are offered (profit and loss, balance sheet, cash flow) for the past two years when AEI was part of FLP, and projections for the next five years an independent. Underpinning these projections are assumptions about the future size of the industry and AEI's share of that industry. Along with this information is a short profile of the company, accompanied by a table of organization showing the present structuring of the company, and a listing of competitors.

While the information one would reasonably expect to find in such a document is included, the depth of the information and the method of presentation could be improved. For example, having a listing of the names of the competitors does not mean much. One needs to know something about the background of these firms, their present involvement in the industry, and their possible future role. To give more meaning to both the profile of the industry and those within the industry, one should know something about the societal environment in which these entities, as well as AEI, exist.

Concerning the pro forma financial statements, they appear to rest on two assumptions which are seemingly unsupported: the past is indicative of the future, and that AEI as an independent entity will be more profitable than when it was part of FLP. While these two assumptions may indeed be so, there is no evidence offered. One would be more inclined to accept projections about this future state of the world if some reasoning were presented which seemed to be creditable and relevant.

There are a number of inclusions which might be helpful for this plan, not only aiding its ability to sell, but as a device to help firm up and push the thinking of AEI into a "reality corner." Some detailing of the strengths of the company and acknowledgment of the weaknesses of the firm (which will be overcome) would have been good. More about the threats and opportunities outside the company would suggest that the plan really has substance. While conventional wisdom would imply that threats and weaknesses should not be mentioned, they should be covered to lend support to an analysis that is perceived as objective rather than subjective. Also, something about the role of and the commitments made (if any) to and by the other equity holders would be helpful. While knowing who they are and their share of the firm is necessary, it may not be sufficient for a prospective investor.

There are a number of other unanswered questions.:
- The dollar numbers used for "goodwill" are significant in size - are they reasonable and proper?
- What would a ratio analysis show about the present state of the company?
- Is the price being asked by FLP justified?
- Is FLP giving us the whole story about selling?
- How does one know?

While it is recognized that such a listing of questions could go indefinitely, it is important that the major questions be anticipated and answered to insure that the reader feels as comfortable with the plan as possible, and be left with the impression that the prospectus is sound.

Epilogue

This set of three sequential business plans provides us with a sense of flow, a feeling that we know where AEI has come from and, perhaps not as clearly, where it is headed. The identification of AEI's tendency to present itself in a somewhat clinical manner, hiding its "heart", has exposed a weakness that exists in many high tech firms. In order to maintain their focus and comply with the multitude of regulations that govern their business, engineers, scientists, and others who deal more often with materials rather than people may give the impression of coldness. In the case of AEI, this is a false impression. Jack Roselle has, in fact, created a company that is civilized, warm, and concerned for the well being of all employees. It is a company of "real people", although this message does not come through in his business plans.

AEI has committed itself to a quality environment. By the year 2000, they will have reached the ISO 9000 international quality standard, thus opening additional markets to them. This certification process is costly and time-consuming, and carries with it no guarantees of financial success. Despite not being forced to seek out this certification by the avionics industry (which has provided a great proportion of their sales in the past), Roselle believes that ISO 9000 will be an advantage to AEI in the international marketplace. Certainly, a focus on quality cannot possibly hurt the company. And, although not perfect, this third business plan was successful.

In business planning, style is not everything, but it counts for a great deal. Aerotech Engineering Industries, Inc. shows us that good writing and readability help the potential reader to understand and support your project, and may overcome some basic weaknesses in content. Each time you rewrite your plan and rethink your goals, you are likely to be making improvements that limit the temptation to pursue many directions, just because you can.

Dr. Trinkaus concludes that overall these three plans would suggest that there might well be a way in which AEI can improve its planning function. Rather than viewing business planning as something that is done on an irregular as needed basis, narrow in scope, it can be recognized as a continuous iterative process, broad in what it encompasses. All three plans seem to suggest that while this latter approach is the standard operating practice for the firm for its production and operation activities, this is not the case for its managerial operations. While one might well argue that the firm is doing well without this attention to the management side of the business, *the real issue is how much better it could be doing if it devoted as much time and effort to business planning as it apparently does to engineering planning.*

Chapter 8

———————————————————▶

Sales and Distribution:
One a Penny, Two a Penny

Sales and distribution companies focus on the movement of goods and services from the producer to the consumer. This includes both wholesale and retail sales in all types of industries. When a business' primary purpose is to arrange for the profitable sale of other companies' output, they face unique challenges. Their concerns include the establishment and maintenance of distribution channels, seeking out and establishing relationships with customers and potential customers, and continuous evaluation of the products they represent to make sure they are meeting their own standards as well as any industry-specific standards that have been established.

The sales and distribution sector of the U.S. economy blankets all industries, for there are no goods or services that do not change hands in some fashion. And that fashion is evolving rapidly. It includes global markets, even for small business, electronic distribution channels, new market niches, and continually escalating competition. In fact, many distribution companies and franchises find themselves in direct competition with manufacturer's outlets run by their own suppliers.

Depending on the product, the relationship between the distributor, the producer, and the end-user may be more or less difficult to maintain. The role of the distributor as go-between demands a highly evolved understanding of the market, the product, and the competition. A distributor who stocks equivalent products from more than one supplier needs to be acutely aware of the differences, however small, among the different brands and understand what may appeal to various market segments. This is a complex task when dealing with durable goods such as furniture, clothing, and hardware.

If, however, the product is a consumable item, such as food, stationery supplies, cleaning products, or the product described below, lighting supplies, the distribution company has special concerns. Although shelf-life may not be a factor in lighting supplies as it is in food provision, changes and improvements in the technology demand specific inventory control measures and flexible and responsive marketing methods. If your company is distributing products on the leading edge of technological change, careless misreading of the marketing climate may leave you with the equivalent of a warehouse full of hula hoops.

Coupled with this need for market-sensitivity is the ability to read environmental tea-leaves as they relate to your product area. In the case of lighting supplies, energy conservation is a hot button. This *should* mean that reduced energy-demand products will be in public favor. If the economy is also depressed, this *should* indicate a growth climate and increased demand for your efficient and effective product. But it doesn't always work that way, and that is the major challenge that distributors face -- how to keep products moving in the face of reduced or erratic demand that cannot be explained by rational analysis.

One area that bears close attention in the business plan of a distribution company at its various life cycle stages is an emphasis on the formulation of strategy. Inattention to issues of positioning, market, and economy spell disaster for the sales organization.

Case Example #3-- Brite Future Lighting, Inc.

The following plan has some significant pitfalls for you to identify and avoid. If your plan reads like this one, ask youself questions like:

- Is it clear to the reader who is unfamiliar with me or my business **exactly** what my goals are?
- Have I provided an adequate rationale for someone to lend me money (offer me credit, invest in my company, work for me, buy my product?)
- Am I sure where I am going?

Brite Future Lighting, Inc. was founded in 1991 with a startup investment of approximately $30,000. Pretax earnings (less non-recurring major income plus non-recurring major expenses) through 1993 were less than $50,000, as was the business' net worth. At the time this plan was written, the Hammonds projected a 20-30% rate of sales growth over the next five year period. In the first quarter of 1994, they evaluated their corporate financial health as "less than satisfactory."

Their method of setting prices is "what the market will bear." They set a list price of 2.3 times cost, and then allow the sales reps to discount down to 1.3 times cost. In these cases, the reps take a smaller percentage of the sale.

They believe that their business plan was a good guide for development, but recognize the need for better staffing through more careful recognition of skills required for various positions. The Hammonds believe that as they improve their systems, eventually they will be able to hire people to step in and relieve some of the pressure they feel.

Brite Future's business plan illustrates a plan for a company trying to climb out of start-up mode and move to the growth phase. Their emphasis on competitive strategy and industry comparisons fairly shouts "start-up," but their marketing strategy/positioning statement and distribution channels provide a clear growth message. Their organizational plan is in start-up condition as well, and their financials signal a struggling new business. The transition they are aiming for is one of the hardest to make for small businesses; their survival depends on their ability to make it.

Financing Proposal

Brite Future Lighting, Inc.

Ann Arbor, Michigan

Prepared by:

Charlotte Hammond, Chairperson and CEO
February 10, 1993

STATEMENT OF PURPOSE

Brite Future Lighting, Inc. (BFLI), is seeking funding to enable it to finance purchases from its vendors during a contract with the Michigan State Electric and Gas Corporation which runs from January 27, 1993, to June 30, 1993. The amount sought is $100,000 in a line of credit.

USE OF FUNDS

To Finance Inventory: $100,000

Orders for compact fluorescent bulbs will be prepaid by customers, enabling us to keep inventory flowing in up to the limits of our credit lines with suppliers which total $100,000. However, we anticipate needing to reorder at least twice our credit lines during the height of the rebate program, and will therefore need to pay our suppliers in advance.

Overview of MSEG/BFLI Contract

The Electric Marketing Representatives of Michigan Electric and Gas Corporation are suggesting BFLI exclusively, as a supplier of compact fluorescent bulbs and fixtures to small and medium-sized retail businesses in MSEG franchise territory all across Michigan state. (See January 27, 1993, letter from Mr. Thomas Wilson of MSEG to Gary Hammond and map of the MSEG territory, in Appendix.) MSEG will promote heavily the purchase of compact fluorescent bulbs and fixtures during a period from February 15, 1993, through May 1, 1993, and is offering $10 rebate coupons to its residential customers for compact fluorescent bulbs, as well as $25 rebate coupons for fluorescent fixtures. (Rebate coupons in Appendix.) The number of bulbs to be sold has been forecast from 50,000 to 400,000. We expect to get the majority of that business since there aren't very many large suppliers in MSEG territory which does not include any cities larger than Flint. (This is similar to, much larger than, a compact fluorescent rebate program run by Ann Arbor Gas & Electric from February through June, 1992).

In addition, from those retail businesses that already have a source of supply but wish to broaden it, the MSEG marketing rep will provide product and ordering information from BFLI. MSEG is also offering to remove the retailer's risk by buying back from the retailer up to $300 of any unsold inventory between June 1 and June 30, 1993. Profit on these bulbs will be $2-8 each, as contrasted with nickels or dimes on old-style light bulbs.

MSEG Marketing Reps will only receive their bonus if they achieve their quota for demand-side power reduction by June 30, 1993. (Achievement of quota will be measured by the number of rebate coupons redeemed. Their quotas have been set at 5 times the 1992 quotas.) Three MSEG divisions have marketing reps and power-reduction quotas: residential, commercial/industrial , and agricultural. If both agricultural and commercial/industrial reps reach their quotas and the residential marketing reps do not, then none of the three divisions will receive their bonus. The residential marketing reps are depending on the lighting portion of the rebate program as their best hope to make quota, since it has been difficult for them to convince homeowners to replace still-functioning water heaters (the only other item on the residential program) with more energy-efficient ones. Therefore the probability is high that the residential marketing reps will make the residential lighting rebate program succeed.

BUSINESS PROPOSAL INDEX

Statement of Purpose
Use of Funds
Overview MSEG/BFLI Contract

The Business
Description of Business
Goals of the Founders
Market
Competition
Management

Financial Data (not included here)
Current Balance Sheet (December 31, 1992)
Combined Income Statement (D.B.A. and Corporation), 1991/92
Personal Financial Statement as of 2/10/93

Supporting Documents (not included here)

Market
BFLI Brochure: "Headquarters for Energy-Saving Lighting" (4 Pages)
Example of BFLI Proposal
Marketing Handouts for Trade Show
Environmental Conservation Award for Customers of BFLI
Advertisement to Homeowners

Commendations
Certificate of Technical Competence from Harris Manufacturing, Inc.
Ann Arbor Gas & Electric Business Award to BFLI
Letter from Ferric Corporation re: Energy-Saving Lighting
Presentation on 9/16/92

Personnel
Resumes of
       Charlotte Hammond, CEO and Treasurer
       Gary Hammond, President and Secretary
       Office Manager
       Master Lighting Consultant
       Certified Professional Consultant Certificate,
       Charlotte Hammond
       Employment Letter -
       Sales Compensation Plan

Contracts and Agreements
Letter of January 27, 1993, from Michigan State Electric and Gas
Corporation
Minutes of Incorporation
Membership and Service Contract with Credit Bureau of Eastern
Michigan
Better Business Bureau CARE Participant Agreement

Business Description

Brite Future Lighting, Inc. is a sales and distribution organization for
energy-saving lighting products. Charlotte Hammond is CEO and her
husband Gary Hammond is President. The business operates
currently with two outside sales representatives personally calling on
customers in Central Michigan and one independent representative
calling on customers in the greater Flint area. One person handles
inside sales, sales management and purchasing. There is no counter
or showroom. Two people handle office administration and computer
system development and maintenance. An outside accounting firm
provides bookkeeping assistance twice a week.

Typical products sold by BFLI: Fluorescent tubes and compact
fluorescent screw-in replacements for incandescent bulbs, electronic

ballasts, and fixtures and miscellaneous lighting supplies. Deliveries of product are made by common carrier, UPS, or delivered personally by the sales rep. The company does not presently have a delivery vehicle or driver. The products are warehoused in two locations: 10% in a mini-warehouse at the offices and 90% at a contract warehouse.

BFLI began as a D/B/A (Brite Future Lighting Inc.) in May of 1991, and incorporated in August of 1992. Charlotte Hammond owns 100% of the shares and expects to be certified by the Michigan Governor's office as a Woman-owned Business Enterprise (WBE). This is expected to give BFLI an advantage in contracts with the government and with companies which do business with the government.

For 1992, BFLI's sales were $750,000: 77% to commercial and industrial customers, 12% to a 40-store hardware store network, 7% to other distributors, and 4% to homeowners. As of February, 1993, BFLI has defined two divisions: Commercial/Industrial, and Utility.

In the Commercial/Industrial division, the company concentrates mostly on lighting retrofits for small to medium-sized commercial/industrial customers and property-management companies. Our experience has shown that the owners of such businesses are usually able to make a decision in a reasonable time frame; also, such businesses do not generally have an executive devoted full time to energy management issues, so they value the fact that we include our consulting in the sale of the necessary materials. Also, they are not being solicited as much by the competition, and we can sell at better prices and profits.

In the Commercial/Industrial division, we function as consultants, interviewing the customer about his goals, surveying the existing lighting, mixing that with knowledge of the available choices and the applicable rebate programs, plus knowledge of what helps people to see and work more productively, to arrive at a recommendation. Then we develop the recommendation into a customer proposal, using customer software written in-house. As the customer chooses, we can act as general contractor for turnkey installation of the lighting, or just supply materials.

In the Utility division, BFLI provides a compact fluorescent bulb and fixture fulfillment service for retail outlets and residential customers of utilities. These programs are tailored specifically to the products on which rebates are allowed by the utilities; however, the retail outlets particularly may become customers for additional energy-saving lighting products of BFLI.

BFLI is growing strongly; energy-saving lighting is selling well because it provides excellent economic returns to customers. Utility rebate programs are driving the market. BFLI has established excellent relationships with the Michigan utilities and provides expert counsel to customers on how to qualify for rebates.

Our sources of supply are excellent; we have become stocking distributors (which implies lowest or nearly lowest pricing) for:

Vendor	Products
Spencer Ballast Technology, Inc.	electronic ballasts
Fluoro-Fix Industries, Inc.	compact fluorescent fixtures and retrofits
A-One Industries, Inc.	compact fluorescent screw-ins
Bascombe Lighting Products	compact fluorescents and tubes
Lighting Tech, Inc.	compact fluorescent screw-ins
Redline Reflectors	reflectors for compact fluorescents

We are working on becoming stocking distributors for Hilo Corporation (compact fluorescent screw-ins) and Sanderling Enterprises, Inc. (same). We have become a sub-distributor of Philips Lighting through Petro-Mann, since Philips Lighting considered the Ann Arbor area saturated with distributors when we requested to be set up. (Philips has given Petro-Mann a Special Price Allowance which is rebated to them for their sales to us). We also have become a sub-distributors of Osram compact fluorescent through Winchell's especially for the MSEG program. However, our volume of purchases on electronic ballasts and energy-saving fluorescent tubes has become such that we have negotiated exceptionally low prices from out-of-town distributors. It is often an advantage not to be set up as a factory direct supplier of bulbs and tubes because we don't have to represent only one of the big three lamp companies, and we can shop for "deals". For example, we are getting a special price for the MSEG program from Sylvania through City Electric in Kalamazoo.

Goals of the Founders

We desire first that the company be, and be perceived to be, a company of integrity that supplies quality, high-performance products at a fair profit. We intend to develop the people and the organization in such a way that its managers and workers are proud of the company and are personally growing and mutually supportive.

We presently consider all of Central Michigan as our territory. We have significant business from the Battle Creek and Kalamazoo areas, as well as Mt. Pleasant and Lansing. Our goal is to add sales representatives gradually. In 1993 we expect to add two sales reps later in the year to insure our profitability. When all systems are working smoothly, we will continue our expansion.

Currently Gary manages sales reps and handles inside sales and the purchasing function. When our new accounting software and Local Area Network is in place (after February, 1992), Charlotte will take on some of the purchasing and inside sales duties. Gary and Charlotte are the sales trainers; we will offer special compensation to our two experienced sales representatives to do additional field training as necessary.

Our personal goals are to stay with the company as it grows. We prefer the company to remain privately held at this time. We are documenting the processes of the company so that we can consider selling a franchise after 1993.

Management

Charlotte Hammond is CEO, Gary Hammond is President, and Nadine Fortunesca is Office Manager. Their resumes are in the Personnel section of the Appendix.

Prior to January, 1990, Charlotte was an organization development consultant and director of training for an Ann Arbor Company "core group" of Organization Development consultants. Her background also includes three years of sales and customer support as an IBM systems engineer, and ten years of various marketing support/management positions with Infotex, Inc. (a software development and computer services company) from startup to 230 employees.

Between March, 1986 and May, 1991, Gary was selling lighting under the D/B/A. "Brite Lights", and selling lighting products as an employee of Perlights Corporation of Fairfield, CT. His background includes 27 years of sales and sales management.

Charlotte has primary responsibility for administration, as well as financial decision-making, including negotiating insurance, managing and signing payroll, banking, and negotiating with leasing and other sources of capital. She also develops and maintains software systems, such as the BFLI Lighting Recommendations Systems and a customer inventory control subsystem.

Gary's role in the daily business of BFLI includes inside sales, managing outside sales, purchasing, and preparing bids. He is a member of the Illuminating Engineering Society.

Both Charlotte and Gary share responsibility for hiring and firing. They will also share the sales training function as new people are hired.

Nadine manages the accounts payable and accounts receivable functions, as well as inventory control. As new office people are hired, they will report to her.

Mom and Pop are running Brite Future Lighting, just as they did Quick Scan Inventory Systems in Chapter 6. Their enthusiasm and energy are inspiring, but the sheer number of tasks and variety of demands on their time suggest that they might not be able to accomplish their ambitious goals.

Joseph Stasio, chairman of the Marketing Department at Merrimack College and founder of nine different sales/service companies, says that "…this plan has several weaknesses. The development of the management section reflects an organization still being run by the "seat of the pants" method of management. With the exception of the three outside sales representatives, Charlotte and Gary Hammond are totally responsible for all other facets of the day to day management of the business (aside from the accounts payable and receivable bookkeeping handled by Nadine). With sales projected to increase

120 percent in 1993, from $751,000 to $1,649,047, it is questionable whether this "mom and pop" style of management will be sufficient to guide the organization to this end. Other key people are needed as an organization grows to help share the managerial burdens and ensure objectives are met and hopefully surpassed in a stabilized manner. If these people do not exist within the present organizational structure, then they should be recruited vigorously. At a minimum the Hammonds should recruit a full-time office manager to relieve Charlotte of all those duties. This would free both her and Gary to focus on marketing, sales training, and customer service, which are indeed the keys to BFL's future success. Even if the Hammonds do not believe this is financially do-able right now, their business plan should reflect the future need for more professional management and when and how it will be accomplished.

The relationship between BFL's sales representatives and M.S.E.G. marketing representatives is unclear. It appears that M.S.E.G. is doing all the marketing, promotion, and selling with BFI sales representatives playing a minor role. The profit margin on the sale of these bulbs from the M.S.E.G. contract is $2-8 each. This is a broad range and could have a significant impact on BFL's bottom line. Since this contract is the main reason for the funding request, management should clarify this contractual relationship to ensure they are maximizing the sales/profit potential of this endeavor.

Management intends to add two sales representatives later in the year. However, the contract with M.S.E.G. is for the first half of the year, when they expect a substantial increase in sales. For examples sales are forecast to increase to $119,970 in February from $36,000 and then by May to increase to $155,938. Will the sales representatives they have now be able to support the increase? The business plan should answer this question.

In addition to the management section, the plan should have an organization section that identifies the structure of the business, the relationship of all the functional areas of the venture to each other and how management fits in this structure. This is particularly important if the Hammonds follow through with the idea of franchising.

The Market

Energy-saving lighting is usually considered to be a niche market within electrical wholesaling and supply (SIC 5063), but we believe it is a major market in the early stages of development. "Some distributors fear if they don't start selling energy-efficient equipment, they will lose yet another market to the specialists." (Quote from

A Passion for Planning

Dean Holstein, Associate Editor, *Electrical Wholesaling,* December 1991, page 42).

Brite Future Lighting, Inc., sells directly to the commercial/industrial/institutional end-user as well as to contractors, other electrical distributors, and to retailers for resale. We pursue the broad market of general lighting for offices, industry, warehousing, and multi-unit residential users, as well as exterior lighting. We are not pursuing specialty markets such as theatrical, retail customer display, or special effects lighting. Therefore our customers are those companies and institutions interested in saving money on their lighting electricity, and/or improving the environment, and/or improving the quality of light for their workers. "Quality of light", and its effect on productivity and comfort, is our other specialty; usually there is a good tie-in with energy-saving lighting.

Lake Erie Power Corporation has forecast that their rates for electric power will rise from 19-25% in the next two years; at those rates and with similar rates hikes from others utilities, all utility customers are beginning to see the need to save energy. Under a mandate from the Michigan Public Service Commission, public utility companies in the state all have established "demand-side management" departments to persuade customers to reduce their demand for electric power, using rebate programs to provide incentives. Thus the market for energy-saving lighting is virtually unlimited. Few businesses or contractors are well acquainted with the energy saving lighting choices which fit their situation, so they need to turn to a knowledgeable supplier like BFLI.

The market for non-residential energy-saving lighting retrofits is literally all of the businesses and institutions in the country. Despite the current sluggish economy, market conditions favor the success of Brite Future Lighting, Inc. It could be termed a seller's market, in that energy-saving lighting products are new, not widely available, and not under the severe price pressures of mature markets.

In a recession, people desperately need to save money. BFLI shows businesses how to cut lighting electricity expenses. A customer with 100 flood lamps, for example, could save $10,000 over the 10,000 hour life of the retrofit at a cost of just $1,100. The expense saved can be translated into equivalent sales which would be needed to bring that much cash into the company. For instance, for a company with net margin of 5% on sales, an electricity savings of $10,000 per year is equivalent to sales of $2000 over ten years -- less than the lifetime of many lighting retrofit measures. In addition to saving them money on their lighting electricity bill, we often reduce the number of ballasts and tubes and/or number of bulbs, which cuts down on maintenance and air conditioning costs as well.

Competitors

We are considered part of SIC 5063, Electrical Apparatus and Equipment. Our competitors are either electric supply house or "energy companies" specifically targeting one aspect of energy-saving lighting equipment. Using the Dun & Bradstreet 9/91 "Microcosm" database for the Ann Arbor area, we found 24 of the 106 companies listed under SIC code 5063 were electric supply houses or energy specialists. Eight of those are small businesses of $1,000,000 or less in annual sales; eight are businesses of $1-$5,000,000 in annual sales, and six are businesses with sales greater than $5,000,000. (Two did not specify annual sales.)

Comparisons with BFLI are difficult to make because our competitors' annual sales figures include wire, conduit, motors, controls, switchgear, and much else -- 70% of which is unrelated to lighting -- and energy-saving lighting is a small part of lighting as a whole. *Electrical Wholesaling's* research shows that in Michigan, Wisconsin, and Pennsylvania both standard and energy-saving ballasts and " lamps" (tubes and bulbs) account for less than 10% of a typical distributor's business. However, the great majority of what we sell is the energy saving fraction of the lighting ten percent.

Also, as far as size and expertise are concerned, according to the US Government Census of Wholesale Trade, the average electric supply house location or branch has 12 employees who make more than 95% of their sales in products other than energy-saving lighting. We have five employees now (and will have seven) who handle only energy-saving lighting. So, we believe that we are larger and more versatile in energy-saving lighting than most of our competitors, although their large overall volume can sometimes still give them a price advantage over us.

The traditional electric supply business doesn't offer a payback to the user, whose only hope is to pay the lowest possible price for the product. As a result, the electric supply house industry generally operates with unusually low profit margins. "During the current recession, price competition has become fierce, distributors report, resulting in thinner margins and profits. In fact, for 1991 distributors recorded the lowest net profit before taxes in at least 20 years -- 1.75%." (*Electrical Wholesaling,* 11/92, page 21). By comparison, our net profit before taxes for the year 1992 is 6.8%. We account for this by noting that prices for energy-saving lighting products are supported by utility rebates, relative lack of competition, and the presence of a payback removing some of the price pressure.

While energy-saving lighting does offer a payback in lower electricity bills to the user, the vendor must understand the technology so he can educate the buyers and find an appropriate solution for the buyer's particular situation. This so far seems not to have appealed to most of the commodity-oriented electric supply houses. We believe that generally the electric supply houses are responding to bids sent to them, rather than developing the energy-saving lighting market by actively proposing retrofits to their customers.

Other competitors are the small "energy companies" which have sprung up, targeting one technology (usually reflectors for fluorescent tubes). These businesses often provide the cost analysis of payback to the user, as we do. However, energy companies look at every potential retrofit as an application for the one type of system they promote. Because the application is often inappropriate, utilities and end users have come to distrust such companies.

We, on the other hand, have carefully positioned ourselves as a *lighting supply house,* with a broad variety of technologies -- over 400 line items which we have carefully chosen, testing many of them to prove their capabilities. (Manufacturers' claims are often not supported by real world results.) We consult with our customers instead of pushing one particular line, since we have many lines and many approaches. We educate our customers so they can see their options and choose the appropriate products for their situations. We have not heard of any other company taking an approach similar to ours. Please see the BFLI Brochure in the Market section of the Appendix for a compete listing of technologies we provide.

Recognition has followed this approach. In the fall of 1991, the Ann Arbor Gas and Electric Corporation's Demand-Side Management Department invited Brite Future to present the state of the art in energy-saving lighting to their marketing engineers, and forty-nine engineers attended with many appreciative comments. A month later, the Illuminating Engineering Society awarded a recognition plaque to BFLI for the same presentation to the largest property manager/owner, and two of its large downtown tenants. A letter of commendation from that presentation appears in the commendations sections of the Appendix.

This section provides us with a picture of BFLI's market and competition that may be more optimistic than realistic. It's difficult to give credence to their claim of uniqueness in positioning themselves as a "lighting supply house" and therefore different from other energy-efficient lighting providers. Companies of this nature abound in other parts of the United States, and it seems unlikely that they are missing from the midwest. Perhaps the Hammonds need to do a bit more research on the competition in the wider marketplace in order to test the effectiveness of their current marketing position.

Prof. Stasio expresses some optimism about this part of the plan, but he continues to have reservations overall. He says, "The Company's vendors and their relationship to BFLI are well developed. Also, BFLI has a good plan to strengthen these relationships in the future. Their product line is well defined and reflects both their positioning strategy as well as the nature of the markets in which they compete. All are important elements of a successful guide, but other such elements are missing.

A good guide needs a destination. Clear goals and objectives are necessary for a plan to develop a sound course of action. This plan lacks both. In the goals of the founders section reference is made to the kind of company they want to create. It lacks specificity. Most companies want to be perceived as having integrity to supply quality products at a fair price, and being ethical and nurturing with their employees and customers. This is not enough.

A guide evolves from sturdy goals and objectives. They, in turn, are a product of good mission statement for the business. The mission statement answers the question, what business are we in? The Hammonds need to answer this question.

One of the goals stated was the possible franchising of the operation. This goal seems too uncertain and is not adequately reflected in the plan. If they intend to do this, then they must plan for it. As stated, their personal goals seem congruent with the business goals. This is a healthy sign as it suggests management continuity, over time.

BFLI's plan does not reflect how they intend to achieve 120 percent sales growth in 1993. The plan lacks a marketing strategy. Their market is segmented as follows:

Commercial	77%
40 Store hardware network	12%
Other distributors	7%
Home owners	4%
Total	100%

Will sales growth reflect this breakdown?
Will it change? How?
Will resources be deployed differently to achieve this growth? How?

Management is structuring their sales efforts into two divisions: commercial/industrial and utility. How will the market segments above fit into these two divisions? It appears that all except the homeowner segment will fall into the commercial/industrial, which accounts for 96 percent of sales. It also appears that one division will support homeowners' utility segments and 4 percent of sales. That raises some interesting questions. Does the company need a separate division to support 4% of sales? Will most of the sales growth occur in this division and require more resources than planned?

The contract with M.S.E.G. appears concentrated in this utility segment which suggest extraordinary sales activity and growth in 1993. Also in the commercial/industrial division, more consulting services will be required for customers to determine lighting needs for energy conservation and cost containment.

How does BFLI address these issues? By developing a sound marketing strategy section in their business plan, the Hammonds will know what are their long term strategic goals, their short-term tactical objectives, and most importantly - how to achieve them. It will also help determine how much it will cost and how long it might take.

This is the more critical element of this business plan. All weaknesses in planning will be uncovered in the financial section, because it is where all the quantitative values are placed on the qualitative issues and assumptions made in the plan. BFLI's plan is particularly weak in this area. The purpose of this plan is to raise $100,000 to finance inventory. The orders are prepaid by customers but because BFLI anticipates ordering at twice the $200,000credit line during the height of the rebate program, the money is needed to pay suppliers. The justification for the line of credit ($100,000) seems to beg the question of the credit relationship between BFLI and both its customers and suppliers. If sales are brisk and inventory control appropriate, then the existing credit relationship should be sufficient to support the increased level of activity. But let's assume it is not. BFLI does not adequately establish the need for money nor its ability to repay.

The forecast of additional bulbs for this contract with M.S.E.G. which will run from January 27 to June 30, 1993, is between 50,000 and 400,000 units. That is a very wide spread. In addition BFLI expects to sell the majority of those bulbs. What is the majority? Is it an absolute majority of between 51% to, say, 90%, or is it a relative majority between several companies of, say, 25% to 40%. What number are we using to calculate this forecast? Close to the low side of between 50,000 to 100,000 or closer to the high side of between 300,000 to 400,000? With the profit on these bulbs of $2-8 each the answers to these questions will have a major impact on revenue and profits which, when taken together, are the basis for judging the efficacy of the loan request.

Sales for 1992 were $751,000 and net profit was 6.8 percent or $51,068. After accounting for the line of credit and the additional sales generated by the contract, sales are forecasted to be $1,649,047 but net profit falls to 1 percent or $24,621. Without notes and an explanation of the planning assumptions that were used to calculate these statements, it is difficult to understand how this additional business activity is going to help BFLI.

Epilogue

This plan was written as a financing proposal and business "steering" document. This is not Brite Future Lighting, Inc.'s startup plan, but was meant to help them guide their business' growth. The plan is presently being rewritten to reflect more accurately the current conditions under which the Hammonds are operating.

In fact, the Hammonds did obtain a $50,000 line of credit from a commercial bank based on this business plan. The banker suggested that the Hammonds apply for a loan through the Small Business Administration, but paperwork delays slowed the application process until the funding year ran out. The following year, the Hammonds experienced a severe downturn in business, and they were unwilling to present their financials to the SBA. They have continued to finance BFLI through credit cards rather than the SBA or commercial bank loans.

As of 1997, their plans for expansion have not materialized. On the contrary, they have reduced their workforce to four employees including themselves, from their high of seven.

The failure of a startup is not unusual. Nonetheless, it is painful to watch people with a good idea, enthusiasm, and skill fail to meet their objectives due to misreading the market, misinterpreting the potential of their product, ineffective strategizing, and betting against a rising economy. The bootstrapping method of financing has its serious downside, evident when the use of personal credit cards outstrips the ability to repay the high interest short term loans. A careful and close look at their plan could have protected the Hammonds and their employees from some of the effects of extreme optimism in the face of facts to the contrary. Business plans can guide the entrepreneur to cutting losses early.

Chapter 9

➤

Business Services:
Getting By With a Little Help...

"Business services" encompasses a wide variety of activities ranging from advertising to xerography, and including everything in between. One of the fastest growing business service areas is the provision of human resource programs by management consulting firms. An increased focus on productivity coupled with a perceived increase in the stresses of life (including such things as substance abuse, marital and/or family problems, addictions of all sorts, and legal entanglements) has encouraged the rapid expansion of this service sector. Employers have become more and more sensitive to the expense of maintaining an employee who is not working to capacity as a result of personal problems. Substance abuse, for example, results in increased absenteeism, higher usage of medical benefits, increased likelihood of filing a worker's compensation claim, as well as higher incidence of accidents, both on and off the job. Programs that can alleviate some of the costs to the employer have therefore gained considerable popularity. As of the mid-1990's, over 50 percent of companies with more than 750 workers and 15 percent of companies with between 15 and 99 workers have had access to services provided through these human resource firms.[i]

Some of the providers of human resource programs are professional groups of therapists, social workers, and psychologists who offer hands-on programs through EAP's (employee assistance programs). Other providers are consultants who refer employees to therapists, social workers, and psychologists. Still others perform many additional outsourced human resource functions, including the design and administration of benefits and compensation plans, recruitment and testing of new hires, or outplacement of downsized workers.

While some of these services are still provided internally for large corporations, most are outsourced to specialists. There are several models for these external EAP's. The firm featured here presents itself as an established and desirable business property that has fulfilled its promise to the current owner. The business decisions the company's owner faces are different from any others we've examined in this book.

As you consider the plans that follow, watch out particularly for the differences in service oriented plans from those of production companies. If your business provides a service, you will want to ask yourself the kinds of questions that James Butler has had to confront:

- How can I frame my services to make them appeal to the widest possible audience?
- What is the most cost-effective way to deliver my services?
- What is my customer likely to want tomorrow?
- How can I keep my skills and abilities one step ahead of my customers' demands?
- What is happening on the socio-political scene that may affect my profitability?

Business service providers will want to take particular care to focus their plans on the evolving needs of their clients. Social and economic evolution are the keys to a service provider's success; sensitivity to environmental changes can make or break this kind of business. Butler has had to adapt the services he provides in order to maintain his client base. His flexibility is among his greatest assets.

Case Example #7 - Personnel Programs, Inc.

According to James Butler, "no one understands the service industry." It is therefore "impossible," or very nearly so, to raise capital for expansion and growth. Despite having many large and lucrative accounts, Butler believes that Personnel Programs, Inc. (PPI) has a limited future as a result of lack of funding. Founded in 1981, by 1993 Butler had achieved annual sales in excess of $2.5 million, and projected more than $5 million in 1997, all from an initial grubstake of $250 and "blood, sweat, and tears."

Three of PPI's business plans follow. You will be able to see a clear progression from the 1993 plan through the 1994 update to the 1995-97 projections. As you read, take special note of PPI's development. In 1993, James Butler's plan focused on the need for expansion capital. He wasn't looking for much, only $600,000, to finance advances in technology. But these dollars were critical to his continued growth. Having obtained the needed financing, Butler's intermediate plan suggests either to acquire other EAP's or to be acquired by a larger entity as a means to further growth. Although we are not made aware at this stage of what negotiations have taken place, we begin to suspect that big changes are in the offing.

By the third plan, it is clear that Butler is ready for acquisition, and has carefully and skillfully planned this transition. Beginning with his 1993 business plan (Plan #1), we see an emphasis on improvement of information systems. This plan devotes considerable space to developing a case for more sophisticated computer technology in the interests of both improving profitability and of maintaining and attracting a strong customer base. Butler shows a clear concern about the inroads that managed care is making in his marketplace and wants to assure his own stable position for the future. He does this, in part, through innovation in technology and in the method of service delivery.

Personnel Programs, Inc.

offices in San Francisco, San Diego, Las Vegas

1993 Business Plan

Executive Summary

Personnel Programs Inc. is one of the largest independent employee assistance programs in the United States and is a leader in the field. PPI provides a full range of support services to our accounts and their employees (our "clients") designed to increase productivity through decreasing the effects of stress, addiction, mental health, and work/family balance in the workplace. This plan is a "living" document that reflects a commitment to, and recognition of, changes in our market and in our need to respond to those changes.

With accounts ranging in size from small local firms that are members of the Chamber of Commerce to national networks, our clinical and account service staff interact regularly with employees who need assistance and with key management personnel to ensure that we are meeting their expectations. Our growth through the years has resulted in annual billings in excess of $2,500,000 and will continue to increase as we bring new services and techniques to the workplace.

To continue to develop, market, and implement these new services, PPI needs more sophisticated computer technology and marketing tools (or resources). For instance, changes in insurance coverage, as processed currently, cause valuable account services and clinical time to be diverted from actual service to clients. We believe that by upgrading our current system, purchasing additional computers, and training all staff, we can improve our productivity by a factor of 20%. The system must communicate directly with companies providing managed care, so that together, we give a total product to the accounts we serve. Marketing efforts require improved research, sales targeting, new product development, and material and training.

Changes of the magnitude necessary require an investment of approximately $600,000. We have established a set of goals and objectives as the keystone of our business plan. Management has committed the resources and support necessary to achieve them and to move PPI forward. Because of the increased performance resulting from the changes and our sales efforts, this sum will be repaid from operations over a five year period.

The 1993 plan also emphasizes the changes in the EAP marketplace and recognizes its own role in regionalized service provision. According to D. Keith Ferrell, founder of a similar operation in Pennsylvania, "PPI's initiatives for future growth are both proactive and aggressive in nature and scope. The development of "joint ventures", "sub-contracting with health insurers" and "developing a hot-line service for multi-employer trusts" is quite innovative for a company that prioritizes regionalization."

A well functioning EAP can assist employers in reducing absenteeism, retaining valuable employees, and reducing healthcare expenditures. PPI's plan must, and does, provide the framework for growth because:
1.   any organization that is run soundly must have a sense of where it came from, where it is today, and where it wants to go, and
2.   must understand the effects on it caused by the changing nature of the marketplace.

Changes provide stress. Today, we find the workplace changing through increased computerization and restructuring. Employers and, therefore, their employees are being forced to provide products and services at lower costs. Potential loss of jobs through international trade agreements and the need to meet the demands of a global marketplace are also key elements of change. On the home front, dual career families mean less time available for raising children or caring for family elders. A dangerous spiral can result as increased stress levels cause decreases in productivity. The EAP has a major role to play in helping management and the employees manage (or alleviate) these pressures.

External factors are also at work to change the EAP market. In recent months, publicly traded firms are consolidating EAP's to shrink the competition and become all things to client firms. Competition also comes from non-profit agencies and hospitals, which provide EAP services as "loss leaders" for their clinical services. Balancing the provision of local service and regional knowledge with national coverage is becoming increasingly necessary.

As we analyzed the changing market, we developed and evaluated several strategies for growth. Two possible models for long term success stood out: a strong regional system under common ownership or a strong local provider. Our business plan works to position PPI under either scenario.

THE EAP MARKETPLACE

We are faced with a complex competitive situation in which mergers, acquisitions, and new organizations offer similar or differently structured programs to our own.

PPI remains one of the largest privately owned EAP companies in the country. Human Affairs International was purchased by Aetna four years ago. Personal Performance Consultants (PPC) was purchased by Medco Containment Services in 1992. The next two largest organizations were pooled with a mental health Preferred Provider Organization in 1988 to form Managed Health Network (in which Morgan Stanley currently has a major position). United Health Care in Minneapolis recently purchased The Institute for Human Services, an east coast EAP.

Perhaps our greatest challenge is to compete with such fiduciary driven entities. More evidence of such activity is the entry of managed care companies such as American PsychManagement and Preferred Health Care into the field by seeking to create viable and competitive EAP services.

Price competition comes from EAPs owned by hospitals and other nonprofit agencies. The staff often has less experience (students and volunteers are sometimes utilized). The service is seen as a loss-leader to most insurance-billable clients for the institution's therapeutic services. PPI considers this unethical, but it is attractive to short-term cost cutters.

Managed mental health and substance abuse care has been a major developing issue over the past five to seven years. In some cases, this service has eclipsed or overshadowed the EAP. Publicly traded companies have come upon the scene with resources to market a stand alone product. It is often sold to the benefits or finance buyers as opposed to human resources or personnel managers who are familiar with the EAP product.

PPI believes the value of this approach, and the entire managed care product, will decrease as the return on managing the claims dollar produces less spectacular results. This direction is further enhanced as the effects of denying mental health and substance abuse treatment show up in increased medical-surgical costs. The long-term value of the EAP's integrated human resource management approach will become the driving force with managed care and many other services as components.

PPI will be called upon to increase service capabilities in all aspects of diversity, care for aging relatives and primary prevention or wellness. In addition, worker's compensation care management will be a rapidly developing new service. No matter what changes occur in national health policy and service delivery, EAP's and PPI will always have a role to play in assisting the workplace to deal with personal problems of employees.

Some of the initiatives for future growth include joint venture and sub- contracting with health insurers and third-party-administrators (including the State's largest), developing a "hot-line" service for multiemployer trusts, unbundling training and other services such as critical incident intervention for sale. We will continue to explore other joint ventures in related areas such as organizational development and wellness.

The 1994 plan (Plan #2) celebrates the successful implementation of a new wide area network and the benefits that derive from the new computer system, both administratively and in terms of market share. It also celebrates achievements in gaining new clients and training staff to remain competitive:

Personnel Programs, Inc.
Business Plan Review and Update (Plan #2)

July 1994

Introduction

We view our Business Plan of April 1993 as a "living" document that reflects a commitment to, and recognition of, changes in our market and in our need to respond to those changes. This review reflects that philosophy and presents our progress as measured by the original plan and those goals and objectives that we feel will make 1994-95 successful.

Our new computer and wide area network is installed. Introductory staff training is nearly completed for the majority of staff (and will be completed for all by September 1). The training ensures that all employees can understand the wealth of information, ease of use, and increased communication potential of the system.

During 1993, PPI opened 4,000 new cases and served a total of 7,279 active clients. We responded to 55 critical incidents and consulted for more than 600 hours with supervisors, managers, executives, and union officials. We provided 780 hours of training. The data for 1994 is on target to show similar, if not increased, results.

The installation of our new computer system and the training of staff means that all the data which formerly was kept in file cabinets is now on line for rapid access and is shared among team members dealing with a case or an account. By computerizing our account and case files, insurance and treatment provider databases will be centrally updated and instantly available. This eliminates the need for asking the same questions many times and the time consuming search for the current hard copy. It relieves the potential for possible errors due to outdated information.

Internal communications throughout regardless of office location, are facilitated by use of E-mail through a fixed-cost wide-area network which is both cost and time effective.

Counselor activity, as well as new products such as work/family balance are also impacted positively by use of the benefits and therapist resource files on the system.

Our Account Representatives will have the latest information available to them as soon as it is entered into the system. They will be able to share appropriate data with the management of their accounts and be able to demonstrate comparable time periods and even other similar (but unidentified) company performance as indications of progress.

DataMinder, our EAP industry specific software program, allows us to rapidly analyze our workload performance data. This gives management increased ability to detect trends and changes and adjust staffing patterns and resources to meet new demands.

It is evident that PPI is being positioned strategically to make it a more marketable entity through the technological enhancements, training, innovation, and further development of its customer base. The 1994 plan informs us that: We have significantly improved our ability to provide timely services to our clients through the implementation of the Clinical Contact Team. Counselors on the team serve callers requiring clinical action or consultation within set time parameters that are highly competitive on an industry-wide basis.

Accounts Services has made significant improvement in targeting new prospects, proposal writing and account management. New and revised training courses and materials and new or improved products have helped and will help growth.

A full-time sales position has been created.

A new Corporate Headquarters was leased and opened in April of this year. We have room for efficient operations and sufficient space for expansion.

By the time the third business plan is written, James Butler had solidified his position as a mature company ripe for merger.. His stated belief in the 1995-1997 plan (Plan #3) is that the increasingly pressurized EAP/managed care environment is forcing his hand. He must choose between taking a firm stand as a service-oriented EAP or throw in the towel and merge with an MCO (managed care organization). PPI determined that long term success was contingent upon the development of growth models that take into account external factors such as competition from community based non-profit agencies and hospitals in addition to the consolidation of EAPs through public trading. PPI identified a strong regional system under common ownership or a strong local provider as those growth strategies that would catapult them into the next century.
Regionalized provider groups are more effective at delivering health care services due to the lack of a corporate "megastructure" which can be imposing and typically cumbersome for consumers and contractors to deal with. The development of joint ventures, sub-contracting with health insurers, and developing a hot line service for multi-employer trusts (some of the plans that PPI has already put into action) is highly innovative for a company that prioritizes regionalization. They continue to differentiate themselves from managed care on the basis of product and service delivery:

Plan #3
July 1995 - December 1997

INTRODUCTION

Much has changed since PPI's last business plan was written in 1993 and updated in July, 1994.
PPI has met or exceeded all of its operational goals.

- The Executive Committee has been enhanced by the addition of a new Vice President of Account Services and the contracting for CFO services to improve financial reporting and modeling.
- Supervisory staff have been added to allow the Vice President of Clinical Services more time for quality review and planning.
- Every PPI office is linked through a wide-area network and all staff are computer literate.
- In addition to the new corporate headquarters, offices have been added in Los Angeles, California and Boulder, Colorado.
- The EAP field continues to experience consolidation and product definition confusion on the part of buyers.
- INMIC chose PPI to provide EAP services to all of its more than 60,000 employees and their family members, who live and work primarily in Colorado, Nevada, and California. Start-up costs were higher than expected and revenue has been lower than expected.

In order to generate the equity capital to compete in this rapidly changing environment, it was decided to write a new business plan. This plan will project PPI's operations and directions through the end of 1997. Although this is a relatively short time frame for a business plan, it is our belief that by the end of 1997, the marketplace will have sufficiently changed to warrant an update or possibly, a new plan.

THE MARKETPLACE

In the mid 1980s, several companies were formed to "carve-out" mental health and substance abuse claims management from comprehensive health insurance plans. Although EAPs provide some of the same services as these behavioral health care management companies, and they are both integral components of a rational continuum of care, there are several important differences in their products and business cultures.

Managed care firms generate substantial cash flows, especially with "at risk" products and contracts, whereas EAPs are service delivery oriented and subject to loss-leader pricing by hospitals and non-profits.

Managed care services require little account maintenance (the benefit definitions change annually, if at all), whereas EAPs get constant requests for policy consultation on changing laws and social norms, key personnel consultation, training and critical incident interventions.

Managed care client contact is primarily by phone, whereas EAPs provide in-person counseling in local offices and on-site services such as critical incident debriefings.

Managed care deals with paying for treatment of illnesses, whereas EAPs cover a broad range of human resource management issues.

The EAP industry has seen investor-owned managed care companies purchase local EAP firms to enhance the notion that they can deliver EAP services as part of managed care. In some markets, hospital-based and non-profit EAPs continue to dominate. PPI is among the exceptions as one of the for-profit regional EAP firms continuing to grow.

As companies face an increasingly complex road map for survival, success and managing human resources in the 90's, PPI believes that our customers will view us as experts in those areas of human resource policy development and program implementation that are affected by employees' personal lives.

PPI leaves little doubt as to their desired future scenario. In 1993, James Butler sought $600,000 to upgrade his technological systems in an attempt to remain competitive. Funds were received and successfully spent in 1994, and, by the time Butler has written his three-year forecast, the decision is no longer merely to remain competitive. He indicates a need for equity financing with clear intent to participate in a merger:

The capitalization required for the initial computerization was acquired in the form of loans and leases. PPI must now generate some form of equity capitalization to allow for growth. It is projected that PPI will need from $500,000 to $750,000 between now and the end of 1997. The equity will be used in three ways:

Computerization will require between $200,000 and $250,000 for upgrades in hardware and software, a data imaging system to store client files currently on paper and training for staff.

Marketing and sales will require the same amount for the transition to a focused sales staff, market research, sales support materials and upgrading training and program promotion materials used by our accounts.
Working capital.

PPI's primary goal is to stay an independent company until 1997 to accrue the full growth benefit from being one of the few regional EAPs focused on the full spectrum of human resource issues. We are in discussions with several groups, including private investors, BIDCOs and human resource service companies to determine the structure and strategies for potential investments in PPI. These strategies include, but are not limited to, common stock, preferred stock and convertible debentures.

PPI is in discussion with two managed care companies who are interested in purchasing PPI. This arrangement would fit our primary goal if the buyer allows PPI to remain a wholly-owned subsidiary and operate according to this business plan while developing synergy with the parent company in operations and sales.

By the end of 1997, we expect the market to have clarified the role of EAPS. PPI will increase revenue by 50 percent and will be generating a 15 percent profit. PPI will then have a number of options, including, but not limited to: a public offering, sell or merge with an appropriate partner, continue as we are, or develop an employee stock ownership plan (ESOP).

Keith Ferrell suggests that, "As a provider of mental health and chemical dependency treatment services, it is my expectation that PPI will remain solvent and viable in years to come. PPI's business plans make a great deal of sense both from the perspective of practical application and as a model for the entrepreneur. It appears to be a viable company that should do well in the constantly changing healthcare/wellness field. The services that they offer are current and appear designed to be both high quality and affordable. The internal management structure of PPI appears to be organized in such a manner as to be both effective without being top-heavy. PPI's financial projections for 1996 and 1997 are sound and realistic even though they realized some difficulty in pre-tax profitability due to unforeseen account acquisitions and broader based computerization requirements.

As an entrepreneur and healthcare provider, I would welcome the opportunity to either purchase this company or become affiliated with it in some other capacity. I see PPI as being consumer/account friendly and flexible enough to accommodate the special needs and philosophies of diverse economic and ethic groups. PPI analysis is correct when one considers the trend in managed health care to look at providers that can take responsibility for thousands of insured lives and provide for their mental health and chemical dependency treatment needs in a clinically effective and cost conscious fashion."

Epilogue:

As of our most recent conversation, James Butler was ecstatic about the sale of PPI. All that careful planning and years of effort paid off big. By 1995, PPI had turned into a very appealing property, and was being wooed by several managed care suitors. But corporate candy and flowers could not consummate a deal with PPI. A personal belief that managed care may cheat the consumer resulted in Butler's commitment not to sell his business to one. How could he provide his diligently developed products and services through an impersonal managed care company?

When approached by an international conglomerate with interests in providing a wide variety of business services, however, Butler reconsidered. Based on the conglomerate's reputation and its size and influence, perhaps his services would not be adulterated. In a conversation in 1994, Butler claimed that he stays in business, despite the fact that the day-to-day management can be overwhelming, because "Last year we helped over 7,000 people with personal problems. I love to see a [treatment] plan come together."

*In August 1996, PPI and the conglomerate concluded a merger which, in the best entrepreneurial tradition, both thickened James Butler's wallet **and** satisfied his conscience. His mission was safe; he got to remain President; and he smiles so broadly, you can virtually hear it.*

The end-game strategy of business planning is often overlooked. The process of visualization of a goal and establishment of an effective action plan can facilitate any stage of business development, from startup funding through operations development, right into the divestiture of one's property.

---

[i] Cooke, Rhonda. (Mar 1997). "Hotline for Help," *Credit Union Management, 20 (3).* 23-24.

Chapter 10:

→

Weaving the Ethical Fabric
of Your Business

In Chapter 3, we examined Tom's of Maine, and the way Tom and Kate Chappell have kept their mission in the forefront of operations. That is the beginning of integrating your values into your company's operations, but mission hardly describes the whole fabric of corporate ethical behavior. For that, we need to look further. And we need to look at a company that is not known nationally for its socially responsible practices or its family friendly benefits and policies or its specific efforts on the environmental front. We need to look at a small business owner who is not trying to make a point, just a living.

We need to look at Dave Ferrairo, owner of DynaChrome, a metal plating company in Seabrook, New Hampshire. Dave has been in the metal plating business for more than 30 years and is still excited about his work. In 1990, he and his partner, Greg, purchased an established but foundering metal plating company in Rockport, MA and breathed new life into it. With four employees, skill, a great deal of enthusiasm and willingness to work hard, but very little hard cash, the two men purchased a larger facility only two years later. Capacity more than doubled, sales increased by a cool 100 percent, and soon they were seeking additional debt financing to further expand the business.

The only limitation on growth that Dave and Greg were experiencing was the result of space limits – they couldn't expand fast enough to accommodate the needs of their customers. Their reputation for quality work and timely project completion attracted more customers and more jobs than they could handle. Plus, they had considerable skill in plating other than chrome – electroless nickel plating, copper, cadmium and silver plating, and other finishes were being demanded by current and potential customers and, if they had the space and equipment, the two men could put all their skills to use.

Fast forward to 2000. DynaChrome resides in a 15,000 square foot clean, bright factory on three wooded acres in New Hampshire. The original workers from Rockport still commute to their jobs, now nearly 40 miles distant, for the privilege of remaining at DynaChrome. Dave proudly shows a visitor the longest chrome tank in New England – 30 feet of bubbling, ominous looking chemicals, center stage at the factory. Big green rectifiers provide a regular power supply to plating tanks, a series of smaller tanks for other plating processes are manned by several industrious-looking employees, and Dave's son, dressed in the same protective gear as the other workers, describes a plating problem to his dad. A dull hum resonates throughout the hangar-like structure while multiple carefully calibrated activities are conducted. The visitor is struck by the nonstop yet unhurried action – nearly a dozen men, each performing a unique skilled task, with no one who seemed like a supervisor overseeing the work.

"Oughts and Shoulds"

When we discuss business ethics, we are approaching organizational behaviors and themes in a normative way, that is, we are identifying ways in which we "ought" to behave in business. Some of these "oughts" have been identified by the government, and these are called "laws" and "regulations." Laws and regulations derive from social decisions that have been formalized through the legislative process, and these are the foundation of business ethics. Of course, the foundation is the same as the basis, the basis is the same as the first building block, and the first building block is the same as the lowest, or minimal level of appropriate or acceptable behavior. If our goal is to develop an organization that is committed to ethical operations, we need to set our standards a bit higher than the legal minimum. In doing so, it is important to remember that the structure of the organization will define the ethical focus it takes.

As we saw in Chapter 1, start-up businesses naturally begin in an organic format, with undefined procedures, an informal mindset, and a structure that revolves around the owner. Owner and manager are the one and the same. As the business grows, it not only becomes larger. It also tends to take on more formality, it sets less flexible rules and standards, and the structure becomes more complex. The owner and the manager is rarely the same person, and operating systems become refined and more highly evolved. Once the organization has moved to the mature stage, it may be set into a firm bureaucracy, with limits on communication from one level to the next, and with a more mechanistic approach to function. For more about organic and mechanistic organizational structure, you can look to the work of Lawrence and Lorsch (1967).

As companies pass through this process of change, they may develop in one of several philosophical directions – hierarchical (rational), participative (emotional), or transcendent (spiritual). [i] The hierarchical organization revolves around self-interest, and tends to ignore or give little credence to the second order consequences of its actions or the actions of its managers and employees. The focus of such an organization is nearly exclusively on organizational "success," whether defined as industry ranking, amount of sales or revenues, or profit margin. This company will abide by the law, but will tend to seek out legal and contractual loopholes. Its concerns will be primarily to one stakeholder – the stockholders of the corporation. The hierarchical model fits many companies, and is based on the capitalist foundations of our U.S. economy. Some of the best-capitalized and most aggressive businesses have developed in the hierarchical mode, and this can be one way to build a strong financial foundation.

Another route to success (differently defined) leads to participative management, rather than production-management. A participative organization involves employees at all levels in decision-making processes and has, at its core, a desire to look out for the well-being and personal growth of the people who work for it. Success is not only financial, but relational as well. This organization pays significant attention to the physical and emotional concerns of employees and supports this attention with profit-sharing plans and other contrivances, assuming that productivity will naturally follow from willing workers. Instead of managing *production*, as in the hierarchical organization, the participative organization manages *people* and encourages employees to live their values through the organization. Interests of internal stakeholders (employees and managers) as well as stockholders are taken into account, and the unit of analysis is the individual rather than the organization as a whole.

The third model is the transcendent organization, that company whose philosophical direction is broad and inclusive, focused and open to new ideas, mission-driven and committed to transformation. Concretely described, this organization is concerned about production, about people, and about *process* – the way it operates within the world. A transcendent organization is one for which the local and global community and the sense of responsibility to them is a stakeholder, the environment is a stakeholder, creativity and innovation is a stakeholder, and these three stand beside the stakeholders of the hierarchical and participative organizations, with an equal share of importance. The transcendent organization has as one of its goals a commitment to a state of organizational flow [ii] or even spiritual bliss that results from doing a valuable job and doing it extremely well. Some of this can easily translate into a focus on quality, a willing adherence to EPA regulations, or endorsement of OSHA. Some of it can translate into unique opportunities for employees. And some can be seen in the relationships among workers, management, and multiple community interests, including the social, religious, political, and legal implications of these relationships.

It is helpful to note that, in a transcendent organization, profit maximization plays an important role, just as it does in hierarchical and in participative organizations. However, in the transcendent model, profit is defined in economic rather than in accounting terms. In accounting terminology, total revenues less total costs equals profit. Included in total costs are both fixed and variable expenses. Fixed expenses do not change on a production basis, like rent, insurance, and equipment. Variable expenses, like raw materials and payroll, do change. In economic terminology, profit still equals revenues less expenses. However, in this model, expenses includes opportunity costs – the cost of allocating scarce resources that could be used in some other fashion. Some of those opportunity costs of managerial decisions include social impact on the community, the potential for consumer abuse, the impact of pollution, and the like.[iii] "It is the unethical behavior [non profit-maximization] directly related to the conversion of these scarce resources [land, labor, time, capital, and entrepreneurship/creativity] into goods and services that results in opportunity costs." [iv]

Case Example #8 – Dynachrome, Inc.

DynaChrome, Inc. provides us with some concrete evidence of transcendence in organizations. In the business plan they presented for financing the acquisition of the plant in Lawrence, Dave and Greg stated:

The objectives of DynaChrome are, in the short term, to move as quickly as possible in the new facility and to acquire and place in operation the equipment necessary to implement electroless nickel plating in addition to the existing chrome plating operation now forming the basis for the firm's business. In the longer run the shareholders wish to add additional lines of plating to the operation, copper, cadmium, silver and the like. The present client base has a need for these finishes but has to job the work out elsewhere as DynaChrome, in its present facility, cannot perform this service. Additionally, because they are limited by the present plant age, capacity and size, the company is forced to turn away larger orders that are offered but that they cannot, in all conscience, accept because of the constraints of their present situation.

Note the phrases " the present client base has a need for these finishes" and "the company is forced to turn away larger orders that are offered but that they cannot, in all conscience, accept..." Clearly, concern for the needs of the customer is equal to the desire to expand the business. The need for specific services that the company could provide, given adequate facilities, is designed around existing market needs, rather than the creation of a potential market. The "response to the market" approach can be considered retrogressive under certain conditions, however, in an environment of existing need and a response vacuum, moving to satisfy customer desires is the appropriate and wise business decision. This decision also exemplifies the ethical approach – the recognition that each part of the system must fulfill its own purpose in order for the entire system to function properly. Nonetheless, despite their existing expertise, the owners of DynaChrome will not accept large and presumably lucrative orders from customers that they cannot "in all conscience" satisfy.

Further on in the same business plan, the owners write:

The company is known for 'technical' work, that is, for successfully undertaking tasks that are technologically demanding and not for 'mass production' or the plating of enormous quantities of parts in a high turnover, low profit type operation. When a shop gets involved in custom work as opposed to routine, bulk volume work then quality and reputation are of paramount importance. DynaChrome has clearly identified itself as a 'quality' shop in this arena.

It is important to know that DynaChrome customers are varied and disparate, with jobs ranging in size and degree of complexity from heart valves to aircraft engine manifolds. A sense of personal responsibility for the health and safety of unknown end-users drives the quality focus of the organization and all its workers. Although there is great tolerance for mistakes that result in learning, there is zero tolerance for mistakes that result in sloppy work. Dave has invested tremendous effort in preparing the company for its ISO 9000 audit, and he has started the certification process for NADCAP (National Aerospace Defense Certification Program), which will ultimately allow DynaChrome to specialize in the aircraft and aerospace industry, where Dave and Greg have particular expertise and engineering capabilities.

Despite the new challenges created for many industries, metal plating included, by the globalization of business, Dave does not feel threatened by these challenges for several reasons. The primary reason is that he feels protected because the effects of global demands reach him at the very end of the supply chain – by the time the finishing process appears, the parts have already passed through a long series of manufacturing processes. The second, and more substantial reason, has to do with the diversification of his markets. He tells a story about the collapse of the semiconductor industry in the late 90s:

> We did feel it when the semiconductor crunch hit. Fortunately, we were not heavily invested; it might have represented 15 percent of our business, the nice 15 percent. We were told by the buyers about four years ago to gear up to four times the quantities we had been doing. The people across the street put an addition on their building, bought the machinery, and instead of getting four times the quantity, they got nothing. Fortunately, we are pretty diverse in the finishes that we do here in the different markets so it didn't hurt me.

Attaining ISO 9000 and NADCAP certifications is not a simple matter, nor is attaining compliance with OSHA regulations and other safety practices. In order to be certain that procedures were developed and followed consistently, Dave wrote his own manuals for them, refusing to go the easier route of using existing "canned" manuals or software templates. As a result, DynaChrome's quality, safety, and employee manuals are readable documents that include down-to-earth statements of corporate philosophy and values.

The March, 2000 Safety Manual states:

> From time to time, problems may arise that relate to attendance, unacceptable work performance, behavior which is disruptive or is seriously offensive to other employees. To ensure fairness, Dynamic Chromium Industries, Inc. guarantees that no employee will be discharged without having the action reviewed by management. We believe in using a positive approach to problem solving with our ultimate objective being to resolve the situation, treat each person as an individual, and successfully turn the situation around.

What follows is a three step process of verbal warning, written warning, reprimand and/or time off and, in the fact of failure of the foregoing to change unacceptable behavior, a method of termination:

> Unfortunately, Steps 1 through 3 do not always produce the desired results and, in a relatively few instances termination may be necessary. Once this stage is reached, it is recognized that it serves no

useful purpose for you or the Company to continue an unsatisfactory employment relationship.

The responsibility for this process resides with Dave, and it is not a process that he relishes. However, his commitment to DynaChrome and its employees' success leads him to describe the process as follows:

One of my hiring practices is, and this is what works, I try to instill in employees to look at the big picture. Don't look at where you are today in this company; I want you to be thinking of one year, five years, ten years out. And, for the people I can recognize that quality in...we'll sit down and talk to them. I tell them everything I get comes from this company and everything you get comes from this company. This company wants to see our children in good colleges. We want to see our children raised in good homes, in their own homes...every one of those people will own part of this company one day.

This long term, big picture approach works, as turnover at DynaChrome is extremely low. Recruiting procedures have grown from the early "whoever walks in the door and someone's nephew who needs work" to a formal relationship with the New Hampshire Division of Employment, including the posting of listings on their website, prescreening of resumes, and online application processes. Two recently hired employees are working out very well, so much so that Dave has felt confident in making one of them his Safety Officer. For a business in an industry that is among the top five most highly regulated industries in the nation, that is high praise.

Compliance with OSHA regulations can be a burdensome task, but Dave doesn't perceive it that way. Like many business owners, he used to make fun of OSHA and the time-consuming and complex regulations. He made fun until he actually attended the OSHA training and watched the videos. At that point he realized that each safety regulation existed because someone had been injured or killed on the job in the kind of accident that occurred the way the regulations have been designed to avoid. Suddenly, OSHA became a serious commitment at DynaChrome. One hundred percent commitment is not enough – Dave is aiming at 100+ percent.

For example, if an accident occurs in the factory, it has to be reported. According to Dave, "We have to meet and find ways to correct it. What I did instead of just writing the accident report is, I modeled it after my quality program and made that report more of a corrective action report so that my safety program would show a hazard if there were an accident on the job." Dave is establishing a video library in the break room so that all employees can take accidents as seriously as he does.

When questioned about his accident rate, he can recall only two serious incidents in the history of his company. In one, an employee nearly lost a fingertip and in the other, an assistant was knocked unconscious after running into a forklift that was not stored properly. Clearly, his commitment to safety is not based on an existing accident problem, but rather on a philosophy that claims ANY accident is one too many and should be avoided. As a result, he and his team do periodic hazard assessment, which can result in some creative solutions. That long tank of chemicals mentioned earlier in the chapter has a heavy I-beam suspended above it to raise and lower items entering the tank. The beam is sharp at the edges and posed a potential hazard to workers passing by. Dave's proactive response was to shield the beam corners with foam padding, and then test the efficacy of his solution personally, by whacking his own head against the beam a few times. His employees know he cares about them.

The commitment to better than 100 percent compliance applies to environmental protection issues as well as safety. The primary emphasis is on clear air within the factory, as the process of chrome plating releases hydrogen into the air. DynaChrome's 100+ percent EPA compliance record covers water as well as air. They take pride in their recycling process and claim that they use less water than most, if not all, other plating companies. A complex series of tanks and pipes feeds water used in various plating processes back through spray, stagnant tanks, and chrome evaporation. There is no feed to the waste tanks in one process, because wastewater simply does not exist there. Wastewater created in other plating processes is minimized by recycling as many times as possible, and then treating the unusable remainder before disposing of it. Careful use of resources and concern for maintaining the environment have created a factory that is immaculate and nearly odorless, considering the caustic nature of the work. This speaks well to the Quality Policy Statement posted prominently throughout the offices and factory:

To provide our Customers with consistent high quality finishes, at reasonable costs, in accordance with their delivery schedules.

We strive to accomplish this objective by strictly adhering to the Quality System implemented and assuring that we maintain our Policy requirements so that the procedures within will allow only the highest quality products to be released into service.

It is our intent that by practicing this policy and providing the necessary training to our employees, they will remain focused in the direction of continuous improvement.

Continuous improvement is a prerequisite for attaining DynaChrome's goal of becoming the leader in the New England metal finishing industry, the one that sets the standard for the industry as a whole. Dave's goal has not changed since Day One; he and the rest of the organization are focused on reaching this goal, which, at the time of this writing, is within their grasp. They recently purchased a company that is a division of the present New England industry leader, and hope to purchase the parent company in the near future. That purchase would put them in the forefront of metal platers for the aircraft and aerospace industries, able to serve (once the appropriate certifications are obtained), all the major companies such as McDonnell Douglas, Boeing, Pratt & Whitney, Sikorsky, and others. And, if the sale does not go through, Dave's intention is simply to carry on the way they have carried on for the preceding ten years – focused, committed, and improving – until they do reach the goal.

That goal has already served them very well. Conversations with Dave about the growth and development of DynaChrome tend to include statements that give credit to the customers who encouraged his growth, the people who sold them his various companies under terms that made their success possible, the bankers who supplied the necessary capital without bleeding the emerging company, and others who supported his and Greg's efforts. When asked why all these people would be willing to help him, Dave looks puzzled. "They made it easy for me," he responds. Pressed further about why people would want to "make it easy" for him to succeed, he concedes that his success has been built on "a combination of faith, honesty, determination, personality, and hard work." He claims that people have recognized his determination to succeed and that "behind every success, that successful person knows how difficult it was, and if they have a chance to make it easier for someone else, they will."

Epilogue

These, then, are the marks of organizational transcendence:

1. *Self-interest, as in hierarchical organizations, that leads to financial success. In DynaChrome's case, this means profits that increase in double digits on an annual basis.*
2. *Involvement of employees at all levels in decision-making and concern for the well-being and personal development of these employees, as in participative organizations. For DynaChrome, this is evidenced by the*

Safety Committee, with representatives from all worker groups, ongoing training for workers, and by the generosity of its owners towards all employees who have shown their loyalty to the company.
3. *The way it operates within the world – concern about the global community, the environment, and innovation. At DynaChrome, these concerns show themselves in terms of willing acceptance and surpassing of EPA and OSHA regulations, and ISO 9000 quality programming.*

---

[i] G. Vega, and P. Primeaux, "The Three Faces of Janus: Ethics in Management Practice." *Proceedings of the Northeast Decision Sciences Institute Annual Meeting* (1999)
[ii] Mihalyi Csikszentmihalyi, *Flow: (The Psychology of Optimal Experience.* (New York: Harper & Row, 1990)
[iii] P Primeaux. and J. Stieber, "Profit Maximization: The Ethical Mandate of Business," *The Journal of Business Ethics. Vol. 13* No. 4. (1994). 287-294.
[iv] P Primeaux. and J. Stieber, "Managing Business Ethics and Opportunity Costs," *Journal of Business Ethics, Vol. 16* No.8. (1997). 835-842.

Chapter 11

———————————————▶

Resources

This chapter is devoted to helping you locate the resources you may need to help yourself and your business through a transition to the next stage of development. I have divided it into three main sections, one of which is likely to appeal to you more than the others:

- Electronic Resources,
- Hard-Copy Resources, and
- Real Live People Resources.

Each of these sections is further subdivided into various subject areas, including "How to Write a Business Plan," "Business Life Cycle", "Entrepreneurship and Small Business Management," and others. I have limited inclusion in this bibliography to websites that I have checked out and that I am confident will continue to exist for the long haul, books and periodicals that are either current or classics and that I would recommend to a friend, and organizations that have been around for a long time and have proven to provide significant benefit to those who use them. If I have steered you to a "bad" resource or if you'd like to inform me about some particularly appealing resource that I have not listed here, please let me know by email (gvega@merrimack.edu) or by regular mail (c/o Merrimack College, Francis E. Girard School of Business and International Commerce, North Andover, MA 01845). I look forward to hearing from you.

1) **Websites**: Many websites seem promising, but frequently all they do is *promise*, not deliver. You need to be prepared to invest a lot of time in finding the right electronic resource for you. I'm not suggesting that you try any of the many business plan software design packages on the market (you are likely to run into some of these in your web search). They are fun, at least for organizing your material, but the big temptation is to use the templates. The result will be a "cookie-cutter" plan rather than a plan that will be yours alone and will work for you.   You might start with these websites and see where they lead you:

a)   http://www.smartbiz.com
     Lots of "how to" business information on a down-to-earth and easy to
     access site.
b)   http://www.ecrc.ctc.com
     This is the National Electronic Commerce Resource Center and is
     government-funded.
c)   http://www.smallbiz.suny.edu
     This is a non-commercial site for the National Research Network of the
     more than 900 SBDC's (Small Business Development Corporations) in
     the U.S. Please visit this one.
d)   http://www.mep.nist.gov
     This is the Manufacturing Extension Partnership of the U.S.
     Department of Commerce - National Institute of Standards and
     Technologies.
e)   http://www.sbaonline.sba.gov
     Lots of good stuff at this address, including easy to download
     shareware for business applications and one more entry to the White
     House.
f)   http://www.bizshop.com
     Get access to everything, everywhere via this address.
g)   http://fambiz.com/
     This is a wonderful site!   Stories, assistance, business opportunities,
     and more.
h)   http://www.fedworld.gov
     The mother of all websites for government information, access to any
     federal government department including those you will use most
     (Department of Commerce, Bureau of Labor Statistics, Census Bureau,
     etc.)

i) http://www.slu.edu/eweb
This is a nice little website maintained by the School of Business at Saint Louis University, and includes lots of educational information for small business, along with sections about business planning, a bibliography, calls for papers, and several search engines.

j) http://www.usasbe.org
Check out this site for both academic and entrepreneur-oriented papers, information, and links.

k) http://bd.dowjones.com/
Dow Jones produces this bibliography of Internet business sites for research, news, corporate and financial data.

2) **Hard Copy**: The first part of this section includes books and articles; the second includes periodicals and magazines of special interest to entrepreneurs and small business owners.

a) **How to Write a Business Plan (books and articles)**

i) David H. Bangs, Jr., *The Business Planning Guide, 7/e.* (Chicago: IL: Upstart, 1995)

ii) Johan C. B. Bontje, *How to Create a Plan for Successful Business Growth* (New York: AMACOM, 1990)

iii) William A. Cohen, *Model Business Plans for Product Businesses* (New York: Wiley, 1995)

iv) William A. Cohen, *Model Business Plans for Service Businesses* (New York: Wiley, 1995)

v) David Gumpert, and Stanley R. Rich, *Business Plans that Win $$$: Lessons from the MIT Enterprise Forum* (New York: HarperCollins, 1987)

vi) David Gumpert, *How to Really Create a Successful Business Plan: Featuring the Business Plans of Pizza Hut, Software Publishing Corp, Celestial Seasonings, Ben & Jerry* (Boston, MA: INC, 1990)

vii) Brian Hazelgren and Joseph A. Covello, *The Complete Book of Business Plans: Simple Steps to Writing a Powerful Business Plan* (Naperville, IL: Sourcebooks Trade, 1995)

viii) Kristin Kahrs, *Business Plans Handbook: A Compilation of Actual Business Plans Developed by Small Business Throughout North America, vols. 1 and 2* (Detroit: Gale Research, 1998)

ix) Jan B King, *Business Plans to Game Plans: A Practical System for Turning Strategies into Action* (Santa Monica, CA: Merritt, 1994)

x) Donald F. Kuratko, "Cutting Through the Business-Plan Jungle," *Executive Female,* (July/August 1993), p. 17-27.

xi) William Luther, *The Start-Up Business Plan* (New York: Prentice-Hall, 1991)

xii) Mike McKeever, *How to Write a Business Plan, 4/e* (Berkeley, CA: Nolo Press, 1992)

xiii) Harold J. McLaughlin, *The Entrepreneur's Guide to Building a Better Business Plan: A Step-by-Step Approach* (New York: Wiley, 1992)

xiv) Christopher Malburg, *Business Plans to Manage Day-to-Day Operations: Real Life Results for Small Business Owners and Operators* (New York: Wiley, 1995)

xv) Patrick D. O'Hara, *The Total Business Plan: How to Write, Rewrite, and Revise* (New York: Wiley, 1990)

xvi) Linda Pinson and Jerry Jinnett, *Anatomy of a Business Plan, 3/e* (Chicago: Enterprise, 1995)

xvii) Eric S. Siegel, Brian R. Ford, and Jay M. Borstein, *The Ernst & Young Business Plan Guide* (New York: Wiley, 1993)

xviii) John R. Taylor, *Business Plans and Loan Applications that Work: A Book of Models Based on Real Documents* (New York: Taylor-Gray, 1993)

b) **Inspiring, Instructional, and Cautionary**

i) Mary Kay Ash, *You Can Have It All: Lifetime Wisdom from America's Foremost Woman Entrepreneur* (Dallas, TX: Prima Publications, 1995)

ii) Tom Chappell, *The Soul of a Business: Managing for Profit and the Common Good* (New York: Bantam Books, 1993)

iii) James C. Collins and Jerry L. Porras, *Built to Last: Successful Habits of Visionary Companies* (New York: HarperCollins, 1995)

iv) Kevin Freiberg and Jackie Freiberg, *Nuts!* (Austin, TX: Bard Press, 1996)

v) Stephanie Gruner, "The Takeover," *Inc.* (April, 1997) 72-83.

vi) Fred Lager, *Ben & Jerry's: The Inside Scoop* (New York: Crown Publishers, 1994)

vii) Joel Makower, *Beyond the Bottom Line* (New York: Simon & Schuster, 1994)

viii) James Campbell Quick, "Crafting an Organizational Culture: Herb's Hand at Southwest Airlines," *Organizational Dynamics, 21* (2). (1992) 45-56.

ix) Mary Scott and Howard Rothman, *Companies with a Conscience* (New York: Carol Publishing, 1992)

c) **Entrepreneurship and Small Business Management (books and articles)**

i) Frank L. Acuff, *How to Negotiate Anything with Anyone Anywhere Around the World* (New York: AMACOM, 1993)

ii) Amar Bhide, "How Entrepreneurs Craft Strategies that Work," *Harvard Business Review, 72* (2). (1994) 150-161.

iii) Barbara Bird,. "Implementing Entrepreneurial Ideas: The Case for Intention," *Academy of Management Review, 13* (3). (1988) 442-453.

iv) Bruce Jan Blechman and Jay Conrad Levinson, *Guerrilla Financing: Alternative Techniques to Finance Any Small Business* (Boston: Houghton-Mifflin, 1991)

v) William A. Cohen, *The Entrepreneur and Small Business Problem Solver: An Encyclopedic Reference and Guide* (New York: J. Wiley, 1990)

vi) Elizabeth G. Conlin,. "How Do You Know When it's Time to Leave?" *Inc. 16,* 2 (Feb., 1994) 56.

vii) Philip. B. Crosby, "Managerial Arrogance," *Across the Board,* (Oct, 1992) 32.

viii) Gary Dessler, "Value-Based Hiring Builds Commitment," *Personnel Journal,* (Nov, 1993) 98.

ix) Peter F. Drucker, *The Practice of Management* (New York: Harper & Row, 1986)

x) Carolyn Duff and Barbara Cohen, *When Women Work Together* (Emeryville, CA: Conari Press, 1993)

xi) Gerard Egan, *Working the Shadow Side* (San Francisco: Jossey-Bass, 1994)

xii) Max Fallek, *Finding Money for Your Small Business* (Chicago: Dearborn Publishing, 1994)

xiii) Melvyn N Freed, Virgil P. Diodato, and David A. Rouse, *Business Information Desk Reference: Where to Find Answers to Business Questions* (New York: Macmillan, 1991)

xiv) *Encyclopedia of Associations* (Detroit: Gale Research Co, annual)

xv) *Encyclopedia of Business Information Sources* (Detroit: Gale Research Co, trienniel)

xvi) Sara Jackson, "The Great Attraction of Staying Small," *Director, 43* (13) (1990) 64-70.

xvii) Deborah. L. Jacobs, "How to Look Like a Million When You're Not," *The New York Times,* Jul. 10, 1994, Sec. 3, Col. 1, p. 5.

xviii) E.E. Lawler, *Motivation in work organizations (classic edition)* (San Francisco: Jossey-Bass Publishers, 1994)

xix) Jay Conrad Levinson, *Guerilla Marketing* (Boston: Houghton Mifflin, 1984)

xx) Dale D. McConkey, *No-nonsense Delegation* (New York: AMACOM, 1986)

xxi) Allan J. Magrath, *The 6 Imperatives of Marketing* (New York: AMACOM, 1992)

xxii) Sharon Nelton, "Ten Key Threats to Success," *Nation's Business, Vol. 80,* 6 (June, 1992) 18.

xxiii) Rebecca Piirto, *Beyond Mind Games: The Marketing Power of Psychographics* (New York: American Demographics Books, 1991)

xxiv) G. Howard Poteet, *Making Your Small Business a Success: More Expert Advice from the U.S. Small Business Administration* (New York: Liberty Hall Press, 1991)

xxv) Al Ries and Jack Trout, *Positioning: The battle for your mind* (New York: Warner Books, 1986)

xxvi) Senge, Peter M. *The fifth discipline: The art & practice of the learning organization* (New York: Doubleday, 1990)

xxvii) Peter M. Senge, "The Leader's New Work: Building Learning Organizations, *Sloan Management Review, 32* (1) (1990) 7-24.

xxviii) Senge, Roberts, Ross, Smith and Kleiner, *The Fifth Discipline Fieldbook* (New York: Doubleday, 1994)

xxix) Matthew L. Shuchman and Jerry S. White, *The Art of the Turnaround* (New York: AMACOM, 1995)

xxx) A. David Silver, *The Turnaround Survival Guide: Strategies for the Company in Crisis* (Chicago: Dearborn Financial Publishing, 1992)

xxxi) Jack Stack, *The Great Game of Business* (New York: Doubleday, 1992)

xxxii) Robert Stayer, "How I Learned to Let My Workers Lead," *Harvard Business Review, 68* (6) (1990) 66-87.

xxxiii) Catherine Stover, [Ed}. *Problems & Solutions in Small Business Management* (Chicago: Upstart Publishing, 1995)

xxxiv) Marvin R. Weisbord, *Productive Workplaces* (San Francisco: Jossey-Bass, 1987)

d) **Entrepreneurship and Small Business Management (journals and magazines)**

i) *American Demographics* (800 - 350-3060) A monthly guide to trends in U.S. economic, social, and political behavior.
ii) *Entrepreneurship Theory & Practice* (608 - 262 - 9982) The quarterly journal of the U.S. Association for Small Business and Entrepreneurship (USASBE).
iii) *Fast Company* (800 - 736 - 9851) Focuses on new companies and new work configurations.
iv) *Harvard Business Review* (800 - 988 - 0886) Published quarterly by Harvard Business School Press
v) *Inc.* (617 - 227-4700) A monthly publication that calls itself "the magazine for growing companies".
vi) *Journal of Small Business Management* (304 - 293 - 7534) The quarterly journal of the International Council of Small Business (ICSB).
vii) *Nation's Business* (800 - 638 - 6582) Published monthly by the U.S. Department of Commerce until June, 1999. Get old copies – it's a priceless read.
viii) *Organizational Dynamics.* (212 - 586 - 8100) Published quarterly by the American Management Association.
ix) *Small Business Forum.* (608 - 263 - 7843) The journal of the Association of Small Business Development Centers, aims to "help small business owners improve their competitive edge".

e) **Business Life Cycle (books and articles)**
i) Ichak Adizes, *Corporate Lifecycles* (New York: Prentice Hall, 1988)
ii) Richard Beckhard and W. Gibb Dyer, "Managing Continuity in the Family-Owned Business," *Organizational Dynamics* 12 (1) (1983) 5-12.
iii) N. Churchill and V. Lewis, "The Five Stages of Small Business Growth," H*arvard Business Review* 61 (1983) 30-50.
iv) Barbara Czarniawska-Joerges and Rolf Wolff, "Leaders, Managers, Entrepreneurs on and off the Organizational Stage," *Organization Studies* 12 (3) (1991) 529-546.
v) Eric G. Flaumholtz, *How to Make the Transition from an Entrepreneurship to a Professionally Managed Firm* (San Francisco: Jossey-Bass, 1986)

vi) William B. Gartner, Terence R. Mitchell and Karl H. Vesper, "A Taxonomy of New Business Ventures," *Journal of Business Venturing* 4(3) (May, 1989) 169-186.

vii) William B. Gartner, Barbara Bird, and Jennifer A. Starr, "Acting as if: Differentiating Entrepreneurial from Organizational Behavior," *Entrepreneurship Theory and Practice* (Spring 1992) 13-31.

viii) Kelin E. Gersick, John A, Davis, Marion McCollom Hampton, and Ivan Lansberg, *Generation to Generation: Life Cycles of the Family Business* (Boston: Harvard Business School Press,1997)

ix) Hanks, Watson, Jansen, and Chandler, "Tightening the Life-Cycle Construct: A Taxonomic Study of Growth Stage Configurations in High-Technology Organizations," *Journal of Entrepreneurship Theory and Practice 18* (2) (1993) 5-30.

x) Jerome A. Katz, "Modelling Entrepreneurial Career Progressions: Concepts and Considerations," *Entrepreneurship Theory & Practice* 19 (2) (Winter 1994) 23-39.

xi) Manfred F.R. Kets de Vries, "The Dynamics of Family-Controlled Firms: The Good and the Bad News," *Organizational Dynamics 21* (3) (1993) 59-72.

xii) Glenn H Matthews, "Growing Concerns: Run Your Business or Build an Organization?" *Harvard Business Review 62* (2) (1984) 34-45.

xiii) Richard Robinson, "The Importance of Outsiders in Small Firm Strategic Planning," *Academy of Management Journal* 25 (1) (1982) 80-93.

xiv) Edgar Schein, "The Role of the Founder in Creating Organizational Culture," *Organizational Dynamics* (Summer, 1988) 13-28.

xv) M. Scott, and R. Bruce, "Five Stages of Growth in Small Businesses," *Long Range Planning* 20 (3) (1987) 45-52.

xvi) Dennis P. Slevin and Jeffrey G. Covin, "Juggling Entrepreneurial Style and Organizational Structure — How to Get Your Act Together," *Sloan Management Review 32* (2) (1990) 43-53.

3) **Real Live People**: If live human contact is more your style, try the following folks for help. They'll welcome your call or visit.

a) Business for Social Responsibility
    1030 Fifteenth Street NW, Suite 1010
    Washington, D.C. 20005
    telephone: (202) 842-5400 / fax (202) 842-3135

b) Family Firm Institute
    12 Harris Street
    Brookline, MA 02146
    telephone: (617) 738 - 1591 / fax: (617) 738 - 4883.

c) U.S. Small Business Administration
    409 3rd St. SW
    Washington, D.C. 20416
    telephone: (800) 827-5722.
    Local offices can be found in your Yellow Pages. Call them for
    information about all federal government programs for small
    businesses, including loans, loan guarantees, federal publications,
    training, and conferences.

d) Service Corps of Retired Executives (SCORE)
    Local number is in your White Pages, Blue Government section. Free
    consultation with experienced, retired executives in your local area.

e) Small Business Development Centers (SBDC)
    Local number is in your White Pages, Blue Government section or
    contact them through your local SBA office. Provides free technical
    and managerial assistance.

f) The Executive Committee (TEC)
    5469 Kearny Villa Road
    San Diego, CA 92123
    This is just one location of a national association of advisors and
    service providers to small business.

g) National Federation of Independent Business (NFIB)
    600 Maryland Avenue SW, Suite 700
    Washington, D.C. 20024
    (202) 554-9000
    Represents small business interests to state and federal governments
    and is the nation's largest small business association.

Appendix A

The Three-Dimensional Matrix

Three Steps to a More Functional Business Plan

1) Which industry fits closest to yours? Use that column for reference.

2) What life cycle stage is your business at right now?

   Start-Up is marked with an "S" or "s"
   Growth is marked with a "G" or "g"
   Mature is marked with an "M" or "m"

   If a code letter appears in upper case format (S), that specific plan ingredient is a "must have" in your business plan. If a code letter appears in lower case (s), the marked ingredient is highly desirable, even necessary, but is not more important to your plan than other ingredients in the same category.

3) Examine the list of plan ingredients in the left-hand column. Each major element section has two parts: the first part indicates the essentials, and the second part indicates the optionals. Look for both "essential" and "optional" ingredients that fit your life cycle stage, and review them with an eye to updating, improving, or redesigning.

   If your business life cycle code does not appear in a particular column, this does **not** mean that you do not need this ingredient in your plan. The appearance of a code signals that you should take **special care** with that specific ingredient, as it will be one that has a major impact on your business at this time.

This coding system is based on criteria discussed by leading business plan analysts and educators. For more detailed explanations of specific plan ingredients and how to assemble them, please refer to the extensive bibliography and resources for small business in Chapter 11.

A Passion for Planning

Element #1 Financials[i]	High Tech			Sales/ Distr.			Mfg.			Bus. Svces.		
Essentials												
Balance Sheet	S	g	m	s	g	m	s	g	M	s	g	m
Break even anal.	S	g	m	s	g	m	s	G	m	s	g	m
Cash Flow	s	G	m	s	g	m	S	g	m	s	g	m
3-Yr Inc. Projection	S	g	m	S	g	m	s	G	m	S	g	m
Optional												
Loan app. as needed												
Financial History	G			G			G			G		
Investor Prospect.	S			G			G			S		
3-Yr Inc. Statement		G	m			M			M			M
Tax Rets.		G						G				
P & L Statement		G	m	G					M			M
Selected Ratios		G	m			M			M		G	

Element #2 Operations	High Tech			Sales/ Distrib.			Mfg.			Bus. Services		
Essentials												
Product/ Service Description	S	g	m	s	g	m	S	g	m	S	g	m
Design Information	s	G	m				S	g	m			
Method of Production/ Plans	S	g	m	s	g	m	s	G	m			
Locations – facilities/ sales	s	g	m	S	g	m	S	g	m			
Optional												
Competitive Strategy	S			G	g	m	S	g	m	S	g	m
Suppliers		G				M	S	g	m			
Production Goals/Systems		G					s	G	m	S	g	m
QA Indicators	S				G		S	g	m		G	
Industry Studies				S	g	m	S	g	m	S		

Element #3 Marketing Plan	High Tech			Sales/ Distrib			Mfg.			Bus. Services		
Essentials												
Competitive Analysis	s	G	m	S	g	m	S	g	m	S	g	m
Target Market Description	S	g	m	s	G	m	S	g	m	S	g	m
Marketing Strategy/ Positioning	S	g	m	s	G	m	S	g	m	S	g	m
Optional												
Promotions/ Advertising	S			S				G			G	
Pricing			M	S				G		S		
Market Entry Timing	S			S			S			S		
Sales Area		G				M			M			M
Sales F'recasts		G		S				G				M
Sales Budgets			M		G				M			M
Dist. Channels	s	G	m		G			G			G	

Element 4: Organization Plan	High Tech			Sales/ Distr.			Mfg.			Bus. Services		
Essentials												
Description of the Business	s	G	m	s	G	m	s	g	M	S	g	m
Legal Structure	s	G	m	S	g	m	s	g	M	S	g	m
Mgt Structure	s	g	M	s	G	m	S	g	m	s	G	m
Staffing Policies	s	G	m	s	G	m	S	g	m	S	g	m
Org. Chart	s	g	M	s	g	M	s	G	m	s	G	m
Mission/Phil.	S	g	m	s	g	M	S	g	m	S	g	m
Optional												
Advisory Boards	S				G				M	S		
Org. Goals	S			S			S			S		
Admin. Procs.			M		G			G		S		
Licenses, etc.							S			S		
Other Value-Added Procs.	S	g	m		G				M	S		
Int'l Ops.		G			G			G			G	

Element #5 Ethics	High Tech	Sales/ Distr.		Mfg.		Bus. Svces.
Essentials at All Stages						
Principles						
Code of Ethics						
Ethical Audit Process						

Element # 6 Supporting Docs.	High Tech	Sales/ Distr.	Mfg.	Bus. Svces.
All As Needed/ Desired				
Owner's Fin'l Statement	S	S	S	S
Credit Reports				
Leases/Lic's/ Contracts				
Resumes				
Letters of Ref.				
Location Studies				
Projections				
Demographic Reports				
Job Descrip.				
Capital Assets				
Pre-Prod. Orders				

[i i] S/s = Start-Up   G/g = Growth   M/m = Maturity

Appendix B

Designing a Code of Ethics
and
Preparing an Ethical Audit

Nearly every industry and profession in the United States, from the Automotive Parts Rebuilders Association to the American Zoo and Aquarium Association, has its own association or organization, and many of these maintain a Code of Ethics specifically for that industry. These codes naturally focus on the kinds of ethical issues raised most frequently by member practitioners, and provide generally acceptable (to their membership) methods of response to legal restrictions. When designing your own company's code, you will want to familiarize yourself with these industry standards.

Step I:

Determine which group, association, profession or industry you most identify with. Although this sounds foolishly simplistic, this decision can be a challenge when conflicting interests drive your organizational focus or priorities. For example, do you identify your gym as a health-related business or as a personal care related business? A health-related business will likely lean towards priorities identified in the Code of Ethics of the American Society of Exercise Physiologists [i] while a personal care organization will be more concerned with the priorities of the Code of Ethics of the National Amateur Bodybuilders Association. [ii]

Once you have selected the code that best reflects your concerns, examine it carefully. Be as critical as you can, asking question about the kind of ethical challenges you have confronted or have heard about. Test the code on its ability to respond to your problems and to guide your decision-making.

Step II:

Begin to develop your own code, based on the industry standards. Where an industry Code of Ethics will state, "Journalists should be sensitive when seeking or using interviews or photographs of those affected by tragedy or grief" and "Journalists should avoid conflicts of interest, real or perceived," [iii] if you own a newspaper, your own code should define *specifically* what you mean by "sensitive" and by "conflict of interest."

This means that you have to think through each ethical area carefully, remembering that your value system will drive the definitions you provide. This is "nit-picky" work, and demands a commitment that will serve you and your employees well in the long term.

Compare the following industry Code of Ethics with excerpts from a member organization's current working code:

INDUSTRY CODE

Code of Marketing Ethics: Conflict of Interest – not knowingly participate in a conflict of interest without prior notice to all parties involved. [iv]

CORPORATE CODE

Becton, Dickinson and Company hereby restates the Company's policy relating to conflicts of interest, first adopted and published in 1962. This current statement reaffirms the continuing obligation of the Company to ensure that the actions of its directors, officers and other employees are above reproach and suspicion, and provides some guidance as to situations which might bring about a conflict of interest.

It is the policy of Becton, Dickinson and Company that no director, officer or employee shall take any action, engage in any activity or place herself or himself in a position which reasonably could be construed to be in conflict with the best interests of the Company.

The Office of the Chairman of the Company is responsible for administering this policy in such a manner as to obtain disclosure of any conflicts of interest involving officers and other employees and to determine whether they are adverse to the best interests of the Company. The Committee on Directors of the Company's Board of Directors is responsible for so administering this policy with respect to the members of the Company's Board of Directors.

On an annual basis, the Office of the Chairman shall inform the Corporate Responsibility Committee of the Company's Board of Directors of its administrative activity during the preceding year, including the occurrence of all significant events relating to this policy.

Every director, corporate officer and employee has a duty to avoid business, financial or other direct or indirect interests or relationships which conflict with the interest of the Company, which divide one's loyalty to the Company, or which detract from providing full attention to one's employment responsibilities. Any activity which even appears to present such a conflict must be avoided or terminated unless, after disclosure to the appropriate level of management, it is determined that the activity is not harmful to the Company or otherwise improper.

All personnel of the Company must deal with contractors, suppliers, customers and all other persons doing business with the Company in the best interests of the Company without favor or preference based on personal considerations. Such considerations include not only direct interests, but interests of members of the individual's immediate family, trust, estates or others over which the individual may exercise control.

Some situations may be governed by securities and antitrust laws or by other laws and government regulations. It is the policy of the Company to comply with all applicable laws and to insist all its employees do so also.

While all the situations in which a conflict of interest may arise cannot be anticipated, in order to alert directors, officers, and employees to the general areas of possible conflict, the Company has adopted a set of Basic Principles that are intended to inform the judgment of Becton Dickinson directors, officers and employees regarding potential conflict of interest situations. These are set forth in Attachment A, along with more specific explanations of how these principles apply to situations and issues that arise frequently. The company shall review and update these Basic Principles periodically, and recommend any material modifications to Corporate Responsibility Committee of the company's Board of Directors for approval. [v]

This corporate code clearly outlines what a conflict of interest is, who is liable to have such a conflict, who is responsible for administering the code, what the relationship is of the code to the law, how to handle situations that are not specified in the code, and the regularity of review and update of the code of ethics.

Step III:

In addition to specificity and clarity, you will want to include information about infractions or violations of the code, and resultant corporate responses.

This is where your ability to be direct with your employees will provide the biggest payback. If it is clear to the reader that you will be monitoring ethical behavior on a regular and ongoing basis, the opportunities for individuals to wander from your defined ethical path will diminish significantly. This should not suggest severe punitive response to violation; rather it should suggest that there is zero tolerance to violation and little opportunity to bend the ethical rules.

Since the most effective Codes of Ethics are public documents, it is quite easy to review them for examples, which vary significantly in enforceability and severity. Some codes have framed the concept this way:

- Violations of the code by a member may result in censure or censure and suspension from membership in The Society. All reported violations will be reviewed by a Presidentially appointed Board of Inquiry or by the Council of the Society. [vi]

- These standards are voluntary. They are intended to serve as a guide to the kind of agency conduct which experience has shown to be wise, foresighted and constructive. [vii]

- As a remedy the Administrator may order a refund to the customer or repair or replacement of the item purchased. The Administrator may additionally request payment by the company of a voluntary contribution of up to $500 (to a special assessment fund for publicizing the Code) and submission of a written assurance of specific steps to be taken by the company to prevent similar Code violations in the future...In cases of non-cooperation with the Administrator or noncompliance with any remedy, the Administrator may, after consultation with independent legal counsel and notice to the company, report any probable law violations to the appropriate government agency. [viii]

- Failure to comply with the standards contained in the Code will result in disciplinary action that may include termination, referral for criminal prosecution, and reimbursement to Martin Marietta for any losses or damages resulting from the violation. As with all matters involving investigations of violations and discipline, principles of fairness and dignity will be applied. Any employee charged with a violation of this code will be afforded an opportunity to explain his or her actions before disciplinary action is taken. [ix]

Step IV:

Build in to your Code of Ethics a system of review and updating of the code. If the code becomes one of those documents that you give to people when they start work for you and it is never referred to again, you can be guaranteed that employees will not favor it with more attention than you have. Maintaining a functional Code of Ethics requires effort, it requires monitoring, and it requires vigilance. Commitment to the code must come from the top, and it must permeate the organization. If you hand off the responsibility for maintenance of the code to a committee, please be certain that the committee includes you.

As business models change and as your business evolves, it is likely that the ethical challenges that face you will transform as well. The issues you faced as a start-up (presenting yourself as larger and more established than you are or financing your business on your personal credit cards) turn into issues of growth (formalizing equitable hiring policies or providing appropriate levels of benefits for all employees). And when you reach a stage of mature corporate development, concerns about honesty in the face of corporate reinvention or methods of self-divestiture may become paramount. If your Code of Ethics does not provide you and your organization with a solid foundation on which to base your decisions, you will find it most difficult to maintain your idealistic standards.

An effective way to monitor the ethical behavior of your organization is to perform a regular Ethical Audit.

The Ethical Audit

The ethical audit has its origins in financial auditing, a process of monitoring accounting procedures to ensure accuracy and non-violation of general accepted accounting procedures. An ethical audit differs from a financial audit in both its methods and in its desired outcomes.

The hoped-for result of a financial audit is a clean bill of health for the corporate books. The hoped-for outcome of an ethical audit is a clear indication of areas that warrant further attention and concern to ensure the *future* potential for ethical violation. The goal is continuous improvement in ethical corporate behavior, with the recognition that ethical corporate behavior is a process, not a destination. The only guarantee that businesses have of future ethical compliance is ongoing monitoring of the activities of all stakeholders of the corporation or organization. It is for that reason that an ethical audit is conducted on a regular basis, either annually or biennially.

One simple method of ethical auditing is to survey the various stakeholders of an organization: employees, management, suppliers, customers, the competition, and anyone else who has an intimate interest in the success or failure of the organization. This group includes the local and global community and the social, religious, political, and legal implications of their involvement in your company. The survey should cover only those areas with which the specific stakeholder group has significant familiarity. For example, The Body Shop Australia/New Zealand has conducted what it calls a "Social Audit" by interviewing relevant stakeholder groups and analyzing their responses to questions of local importance. The data were verified by an independent auditor and provided direction for the company for the near and long term.

In the case of The Body Shop, the questions revolved around issues of environmental concern (product stewardship, sustainable resources, pollution and waste management), animal protection, and ethical business practices (integrity and honesty, exceptional customer service, level of trust in the corporation, job security and job satisfaction, adherence to corporate mission, and humanitarian values). [x] You will have to design questions that are relevant to your own business.

Levi Strauss & Company has designed a different sort of ethical audit tool. Their audit revolves primarily around issues that may affect the corporate reputation and, due to their very large size, they compare themselves with companies in the same sector or industry, companies of comparable size, and all companies doing business in the relevant marketplace. [xi] Areas of comparison include corporate practices and standards, financial performance, products and services, management, employment practices, wages and benefits, workplace environment, environmental stewardship, and community involvement. A baseline number is calculated for each of these categories, with the understanding that the corporate goal is to exceed the previous audit's number each time the audit is conducted.

A much simpler format is suggested by Lawrence Barton [xii] He provides a 25 question yes/no instrument which covers the areas of policies and procedures, finance, public relations, human resources, operations, legal, and implementation. Some of the questions address core operational concerns, such as "What kind of fact-finding procedures do we have or should be established to ensure that fairness is paramount in our efforts?" and "If one of our senior managers is well-versed and experienced in communicating the ethical standards in place at our company, have we made arrangements for these individuals to visit various locations and offer presentations to colleagues?"

This audit concludes with a scoring mechanism that identifies four categories of achievement – one of serious defects in the company's ethical programs, one of considerable ambiguity or gaps, one that meets many accepted practices but still needs some work, and the fourth in which the company has generally met or exceeded generally accepted ethical practices. This scoring can be helpful, as long as the questions on the survey legitimately address your own business concerns.

There is no better way to design an ethical audit than to do it yourself, using your own problem, issues, and goals. You will be guided by your mission in this task; therefore, your mission is the starting point for all ethical analysis of your company.

Begin at the beginning.

---

[i] http://www.css.edu/users/tboone2/asep/ethics.htm

[ii] http://www.nabba.com/ethics.htm

[iii] Society of Professional Journalists Code of Ethics, in Pincus, L. *Perspectives in Business Ethics*. (New York: McGraw-Hill, 1998) 673-675.

[iv] http://www.directorshandbook.com/market_ethics.html

[v] Becton, Dickinson and Company Conflicts of Interest Policy Statement, September 23, 1997. 8.

[vi] Code of Ethics of the Wildlife Society. http://csep.iit.edu/publicwwwcodes/coe

[vii] Code of Ethics of the American Association of Advertising Agencies. http://www.csep.iit.edu/publicwwwcodes/coe

[viii] Code of Ethics of the Direct Selling Association. http://csep.iit/edu/publicwwwcodes/coe

[ix] Code of Ethics of Lockheed Martin. http://csep.iit.edu/publicwwwcodes/coe

[x] http://www.thebodyshop.com/au/about/newbotline/highlights.html

[xi] "Corporate Reputation/Responsibility Assessment Tool," in Makower, Joel. *Beyond the Bottom Line* (New York: Simon and Schuster, 1994) 302-308.

[xii] , Lawrence Barton, *Ethics: the Enemy in the Workplace*. (South-Western College Publishing, 1995) 352-355.

Appendix C

Business Plan
Commentators

D. KEITH FERRELL

D. Keith Ferrell is President of Ferrell and Associates, Inc. a private counseling center with offices in Wilkes-Barre and Hazleton, Pennsylvania. Mr. Ferrell is also the Executive Director of the Pennsylvania Institute for Rational-Emotive Behavior Therapy which is headquartered in Wilkes-Barre, Pennsylvania. Mr. Ferrell is a practicing licensed psychologist and nationally certified diplomate in addictions treatment with over twenty-five years of applied and clinical experience in the fields of psychology and behavioral health care. Honors and appointments include listing in Who's Who in the East, Among Human Service Professionals, Of Emerging Leaders in America, In Medicine and Healthcare and in the National Directory of Who's Who in Executives and Professionals. He has held the position of President of the Northeastern Pennsylvania Psychological Association, 1985-1987; has been inducted into the National Honor Society in Psychology, 1974 and held the elected position of Board President for the Mental Health Association In Northeastern Pennsylvania from 1990-1992.

Ferrell and Associates, Inc.
111 No. Franklin Street
Wilkes Barre, PA 18701
email: <f102150@epix.net

SUSAN J. FOX-WOLFGRAMM, M.P.A., Ph.D.

Susan J. Fox-Wolfgramm is a faculty member in the Department of Management, College of Business at San Francisco State University. She has a B.S. in Business Administration from the University of Colorado, a Masters degree in Public Administration from Texas Tech University, and a Ph.D. in Business Administration from Texas Tech University. She is also a Price-Babson College Fellow and a Samuel M. Walton Free Enterprise Fellow.

Dr. Fox-Wolfgramm conducts seminars in Business Policy & Strategic Management and Students in Free Enterprise. Her research interests include the analysis of emerging industries, developing ethnic entrepreneurship, government policy implications for small businesss management, and strategic issue management in industries.

Dr. Fox-Wolfgramm's most recent publications are in the areas of entrepreneurship, qualitative research, and strategic management. These include: "Towards Understanding the Developmental Outcomes of Government Intervention: A Dynamic-Comparative Case Study of the Community Reinvestment Act," appearing in the Fall/Winter 1997 issue of the <u>Journal of Developmental Entrepreneurship</u> , "Competing for the Critical Mass: An Analysis of the Success and Failure of High Growth Firms in Emerging Industries," in <u>Frontiers in Entrepreneurship Research 1996</u>, and "Towards Developing a Methodology for Doing Qualitative Research: The Dynamic-Comparative Case Study Method," forthcoming in the <u>Scandinavian Journal of Management</u>.

Currently, Dr. Fox-Wolfgramm is working on a series of case studies for the university-setting classroom related to high growth firms in emerging industries. She also serves as a consultant for the Federal Reserve Bank and as a business and economics textbook consultant for Prentice-Hall and HarperCollins College Publishers.

Dr. Fox-Wolfgramm has received many honors and awards including the University and Dean's Excellence in Teaching Awards from Texas Tech University, the United States Achievement Academy Award, the Dean's List Award, and Outstanding Women of America Award. Besides being a major contributor to many San Francisco State University advisory boards and committees, Dr. Fox-Wolfgramm is an active participant and has held various leadership positions in many professional organizations, including the Academy of Management, the United States Association for Small Business and Entrepreneurship, the Commonwealth Club of California, the National Historical Preservation Society, and the San Francisco State University Women's Association.

San Francisco State University
College of Business
1600 Holloway Avenue
San Francisco, CA 94132
email: <u>sfox@sfsu.edu</u>

James W. Lacey, Ph.D.

Dr. Lacey has a broad professional background in manufacturing, management information systems, finance, marketing, and research and development. As a young production supervisor in a small firm, he led his department to achieve a 100% quality rating from IBM, the firm's largest customer. He also hired the first woman machinist in what had been an all-male machine shop. Moving to a larger manufacturing firm, Dr. Lacey convinced his department to purchase IBM personal computers in the year that they were introduced, and then proceeded to computerize manual tasks, cutting the time required to calculate production plans from one week to four hours.

In 1985, Dr. Lacey moved to AT&T Network Systems, now Lucent Technologies. He was both an implementor and user of a new manufacturing resource planning system. His next assignment was financial manager for a $200 million strategic business unit. Later, as a product manager, he increased profits by careful application of economic principles to pricing and costs. Dr. Lacey is currently business planning manager for a portfolio of Bell Laboratories projects. He sees his task as helping Lucent Technologies create the future of communications.

Dr. Lacey's education has been in economics and management. He holds a Bachelor of Arts from Merrimack College, a Master of Science in Management from Lesley College, a Master of Arts in Economics from Northeastern University, and a Doctor of Philosophy in Economics from The Union Institute. His doctoral dissertation was on postmodern economics and implications for business strategy and public policy. Dr. Lacey is a member of Omicron Delta Epsilon, the international honor society in economics. He is also a Fellow, Certified in Production and Inventory Management, of the American Production and Inventory Control Society. Dr. Lacey has been a part-time instructor in economics and business at both the undergraduate and graduate level, and has published articles dealing with workforce issues and with leadership.

Lucent Technologies
1600 Osgood Street
North Andover, MA 01845
email: <jwlacey@lucent.com>

GAYLE PORTER, Ph.D.

Gayle Porter is a member of the Management Faculty at Rutgers University, School of Business in Camden, NJ. Her current position follows 20 years of industry experience, including technical work in the oil and gas industry, finance and accounting with a Fortune 500 company, and consulting on training programs and employee development. A consistent interest throughout her career has been the desire to develop people and organizations to fulfill potential rather than stifle it. Now she pursues this interest as a teacher, researcher, and consultant.

She received her Ph.D. in Business Administration from The Ohio State University. During her seven years at Rutgers, Gayle has taught courses in Organization Change and Development, Social Responsibility of Business, Organizational Behavior, and Human Resource Management. Her research centers on employee development issues from two perspectives. One view is a focus on individual factors that inhibit development efforts, such as low learning orientation or workaholic tendencies. The other view is attention to the context within which development occurs. Much of her work from this organizational perspective is related to work team interactions and team leadership.

Recent research/consulting projects include work with General Motors, Texas Instruments, The Ohio State University Hospitals, and several smaller companies. Her work has been published in: *Journal of Occupational Health Psychology, Journal of Business Research, Human Resource Development Quarterly, Journal of Business and Psychology, Journal of Business Ethics, Advances in Interdisciplinary Studies of Work Teams, The 1996 Best Practices Handbook for Teams,* and other books and journals.

Rutgers University
School of Business - Camden
Camden, NJ 08102
email: <gporter@crab.rutgers.edu>

Patrick Primeaux, S.M., M.B.A., Ph.D.

Father Primeaux belongs to the Society of Mary, the Marists, a Roman Catholic congregation of priests and brothers. He teaches business ethics at St. John's University in New York. With John Stieber, he has published several articles in the *Journal of Business Ethics* examining the ethics inherent to economic profit maximization. With Moses Pava and Gina Vega, he is studying and researching a synthesis of religious values and business values. He is the author of *The Moral Passion of Bruce Springsteen, Reinterpreting the American Dream: Persons and Ethics* and, with Stieber, *Profit Maximization: The Ethical Mandate of Business.*

Originally from Lafayette, Louisiana, he earned a B.A. in French Education from the University of Louisiana at Lafayette (1971), an M.A. and a Ph.D. in Theology from the University of St. Michael's College in Toronto (1979), and an M.B.A. from Southern Methodist University in Dallas (1989). Ordained a priest in 1977, he taught at Notre Dame Seminary and Graduate School of Theology in New Orleans, directed campus ministry at Cleveland State University, and served as pastor of Most Sacred Heart of Jesus Catholic Church in Gramercy, Louisiana before joining the faculty of the Department of Theology and Religious Studies at St. John's.

With Marilynn Fleckenstein of Niagara University, Laura Pincus Hartman of DePaul University, and Mary Maury of St. John's College of Business Administration, he is a founding coordinator of the Annual International Conference Promoting Business Ethics.

Department of Theology and Religious Studies
St. John's University
8000 Utopia Parkway
Jamaica, NY 11439
Email: primeaup@stjohns.edu

GREGORY T. SIMPSON

Gregory Simpson is currently District Manager for AT&T Solutions leading a project for one of its *Fortune* five clients. In his previous position at AT&T, he managed a team of over 100 management and union employees in a customer care organization. He also has an extensive background in international marketing and sales with AT&T and previously worked in a sales capacity for Canon USA.

He has a Master of Business Administration in Marketing, a Master of Science in International Business, and a Bachelor of Arts in Psychology. In addition to studying in the U.S., he has studied in Argentina, Guatemala, and Poland.

Greg grew up in the Adirondack Mountains of upstate New York where he still enjoys spending time visiting his parents. Greg and his wife Janette live in New Jersey with their two cats, Orville and Wilbur.

AT&T
Room 3W102
300 Atrium Drive
Somerset, NJ 08873
Email: <gregsimpson@att.com>

JOSEPH R. STASIO, JR.

Joseph R. Stasio, Jr. , associate professor of marketing, currently teaches at Merrimack College, North Andover, MA. During the past twenty-five years, he has started nine companies including a chain of pizzerias, restaurants, bedding retail stores, and other service types businesses.

Professor Stasio was the Director of the Small Business Development Center at Salem State College during his tenure there and is presently the Director of the Small Business Institute at Merrimack College. He is also a Research Associate at the Merrimack College Urban Resources Institute where he is establishing business development programs for the minority community in Lawrence, MA. In addition to his teaching, he consults and writes on topics of marketing and entrepreneurship.

Merrimack College
Francis E. Girard School of Business and International Commerce
North Andover, MA. 01845
email: <jstasio@merrimack.edu>

JOHN TRINKAUS, Ph.D., P.E.

Dr. John Trinkaus, an emeritus professor of management, is particularly well versed and practiced in the field of minority small business start-ups and new venture initiatives. His experience includes work with such organizations as the Ford Foundation, the Small Business Institute and the Small Business Development Center operations of the U.S. Small Business Administration, and the Interracial Council for Business Opportunity.

Other interests include: ethnology, over 75 of his social counting inquiries appearing in the literature; executive education, having extensive hands-on familiarity with both degree and non-degree programs; the history of management thought, especially the contribution of African Americans; and emerging practices in pharmaceutical care, in particular their impact on the delivery of quality health care.

He holds a Bachelor's degree in electrical engineering from New York University, a Master's in engineering management from City University of New York, and a doctorate in management from New York University. His other credentials include a professional engineer's license, service on the editorial boards of a number of scholastic journals, and membership in several national and international academic associations.

Prior to entering academia, he was employed full time as an electrical engineer, working on the design and development of military electronic equipment, for a number of firms, including the Bendix Aviation Corporation and the Curtis Wright Corporation. His last position in industry, which he held for over 15 years, was with the Sperry Corporation, where he was responsible for the selection and approval of electronic components and materials for new product usage. While in this position he represented the Corporation on a number of government and industrial groups charged with the responsibility for developing standards and specifications for new airborne and seaborne electronic gear.

Baruch College/CUNY
17 Lexington Avenue
New York, NY 10010

INDEX